With an
eagle's
eye . . .

A Seven-Day Sojourn in Celtic Spirituality

With an eagle's eye ...

John Miriam Jones, S.C.

AVE MARIA PRESS   Notre Dame, Indiana 46556

© 1998 by Ave Maria Press, Inc.
International Standard Book Number: 0-87793-650-1
Cover and text design by Brian C. Conley
Cover photography by Ralph LaPlant
Interior photography by Cyril A. Reilly
Printed and bound in the United States of America.

Library of Congress Cataloging-in-Publication Data
Jones, John Miriam.
      With an eagle's eye : a seven-day sojourn in Celtic
spirituality / John Miriam Jones.
      p.   cm.
      Includes bibliographical references.
      ISBN 0-87793-650-1
      1. Spirituality—Celtic Church. 2. Retreats—Catholic
Church. 3. Celtic Church—Doctrines. I. Title.
BR748.J66   1998
248'.089'916—dc21
                              98-4031
                                CIP

To Mary and John, my mother and father,
in gratitude for Celtic genes
and for the love which brought them to life.

Contents

Prologue:

Why a Celtic Retreat?

There is a kind of fascination these days with a rediscovery of Celtic spirituality. A number of both scholarly and popular books on that subject are now in print and treat the topic from a variety of angles. Although this effort delves into a basic understanding of the rich spirituality of the Celts of old, its principal aim is both to endear their spiritual approach to those who make use of this book and to offer practical and personal application for one's own spiritual journey.

If your roots are Irish, Scottish, Welsh, or possibly English, there is little question for you as to whether you might find common ground with the Celts. Those of you of other European roots might be surprised to know of the possibility of distant Celtic relationships. But natural Celtic connections are not at all a prerequisite for your comfort in their world.

What seems so universally appealing about the Celtic people who lived in the sixth to the twelfth centuries is their wholesomeness. These were well-rounded human beings whose lives were centered in their faith and whose faith penetrated every portion of life. God was immediately present to them; their relationship with God intimate; their lives alive with joy and pain, goodness and weakness, work and pleasure.

9

They were persons with whom all of us could readily identify.

The Celts we will be meeting were women and men, a mix of lay, religious, and clerics. They lived together, in active communities of faith, where life was full and vibrant, and where God was available for encounter at every turn.

Everyone's spiritual development begins with a genuine and personal encounter with God. Sometimes it can be clearly named. At other times a sort of vagueness leads one to suspect God has been present, though one is less certain. When that encounter leads one to amazement, hunger, search, and prayerful expression, the first steps of a spiritual journey have been taken. As it develops, it colors all of life. It cries out for ever deeper relationships with God, with one another, and with our truest selves. It is in order to focus and deepen this journey that we periodically enter upon a retreat. This retreat on a Celtic theme is designed for the same mix of persons who formed the remarkable Celtic church: Christian laity, religious women and men, the ordained. It is for all who yearn to intensify their relationship with God and to live their faith more vibrantly.

A Touch of Celtic History

Knowing a bit of historical background will catalyze our appreciation of these persons of Celtic origin and shed light on some unique aspects of their approach toward God. Actually, the origins of the Celtic race are somewhat obscure, but by the beginning of the millennium before Christ, the Celts appear to have been concentrated in central Europe.

By 600 B.C. they had moved into western Europe as well and populated the expanse stretching east to west from the Black Sea to Iberia, and north to south from the North Sea to the Mediterranean. Over the next five hundred years, a combination of climatic changes and zealous conquerors drove the Celts progressively westward. By about 100 B.C., as the Romans began to invade western Europe, the Celts had become concentrated in what are now the British Isles. The Roman march thoroughly crushed a portion of Celtic culture, but lands which escaped Roman supremacy gave rise to the Celts of the time after Christ.

Britain was the last area fully occupied, though never fully subjugated, by the Romans. The hold of the conquerors was tenuous in Scotland with Hadrian's Wall marking the limit of their invasions. Thus, northern Scotland completely escaped Roman domination. Cornwall and much of Wales were barely touched by the Romans. Ireland lay beyond their efforts. So, while destroyed in the rest of Europe, Celtic culture flourished in Ireland, Northern Scotland, much of Wales and Cornwall, and parts of England.

These events of history isolated the Celts beyond the northwestern edges of the Roman world. This fact was highly significant for the Celtic church, for it put them outside the strong influence of the Roman Church until the twelfth century and allowed the purity of the Celtic form of Christianity to thrive for hundreds of years. However, at the time they became concentrated on the islands north and west of the continent, the Celts were still a pagan people, though extremely religious. As Christianity established itself it wisely built upon their strong religious traits. Some

11

of these very traits evolved into distinguishing characteristics of Christian Celtic spirituality:

- a powerful sense of the supernatural world and of life beyond death;
- gods near at hand, integral to daily life, often feminine, and at times worshipped in triads (e.g., the pagan Bridget was their goddess of creation, fertility, and healing);
- the sacredness of the earth, especially water, woods, and hills, where they believed their gods dwelt and where religious ceremonies were held (notice analogies here with Native Americans, Aborigines, and African tribes);
- a high value placed on learning, literary expression, and music;
- the importance of tribal and personal relations.

In all likelihood Christian belief first came to the British Isles courtesy of the Romans during the second century, though in its inception it appears to have been rudimentary and fragmentary. The first documentation of Celtic Christianity was in the fifth century and was associated with Patrick's well-known conversion of Ireland. During the thirty years of Patrick's sojourn, beginning about 431 A.D., all of Ireland became Christianized. Because Patrick built upon and incorporated much of their existing religious culture, the Irish Celts made the transition to Christianity quite readily, accompanied by neither martyrdom nor persecution. From that ancestry came those Christians who developed and flourished during the sixth to the twelfth centuries. The Celtic church achieved a dynamism and vibrancy that spread not only throughout the Celtic lands but throughout all of northern Europe as the Celts set out on missionary journeys. These are the Celtic Christians who will be our teachers during this retreat. Their successors, who lived between the thirteenth and the twentieth centuries, experienced a strong influence from the church in Rome along with invasion, subjugation, famine, revolution, and political division. All of this necessarily altered their way of life and affected their expression of faith. While fascinating, this latter period is distinct from our present considerations. Suffice it to say, peoples of Celtic origin are still recognized for the strength of their faith.

The Direction of This Celtic Retreat

On each of the seven days of retreat we will highlight a major characteristic of the Celts' vitalizing faith during the centuries when their Christian life was in full flower.

On the first day we will explore the wonderfully warm relationship between God and Celtic Christians. God was intimately present to them in every part of their world and their daily lives.

The Celtic world also included numerous inhabitants who could not be seen. Our second day will dwell on the Celts' friendship with angels, saints, and the living dead, whom they readily encountered and implored. Their sense of the presence of evil spirits led them to invoke the friendly and holy spirits for protection.

A truly distinctive feature of the Celts' lived faith will occupy the third day. For six hundred years the religious, clergy, and laity lived their faith together in vibrant communities known as monastic cities. For the Celts, these monastic communities served as the basic experience of what Christianity was all about. In theological terms, they were the "local church."

On day four we will be engaged with ways in which the Celts gave artistic expression to their faith. Celtic design was mystical and symbolic. They incorporated it on metal and stone works of art and placed these easily recognized designs into the illuminations of manuscripts. A natural poetic sense and a facility with words yielded faith-filled poetry, prayer, and song.

Journey was an important part of Celtic life and translated into their faith life as pilgrimage, which we will consider on the fifth day. Both religious and laity felt called to this journey of faith, which was always intimately related to one's need for asceticism.

Because the Celts were such wholesome human beings, we will use the sixth day to explore how these people were fully alive and how the completeness of their human life translated into holiness. Three specific traits will be looked at: their simplicity of life, warm relationships, and attentive openness to God. The three are proper to every true Christian and especially essential for vowed religious women and men.

A seventh day is offered with the anticipation that it can be used at a time subsequent to the retreat days—as a single day or as part of a number of days. It provides the opportunity to strengthen the graces of retreat as well as to integrate those graces by focusing through the lens of God's passionate love for you, according to the eyes and words of Saint John.

14

How to Proceed

Because a retreat is designed to be a time apart and spent in God's company, the ideal use of this material would be to spend seven full and continuous days in a place away from your busy life. If the ideal is not possible for you, devote as much time as practical on seven separate occasions to being silent and alone with God. Every sincere effort to seek God will delight that Holy One and yield grace, whether recognized at that moment or later in retrospect.

For each day, a reflection on the theme will be offered to assist in your understanding of a specific quality of Celtic spirituality. Ask God to open your heart to new insights and graces. Then read the material slowly and reflectively. If during that time you sense the desire to stop to pray, do so.

The reflection is followed by a number of scriptural references which are related to the day's theme. There are too many for any one day, but there are enough for you to choose three or four which appeal and to make them the springboard for prayer. If you have the leisure for full days of retreat, you may want to use one passage of scripture for each of your times of prayer.

On each day questions are posed for your reflection. Perhaps you can think about these as you do other things—take a walk, sit in the garden, do household chores, eat your meals. But you will also want to bring them to prayer, for your answers should open avenues for conversations with God and offer hints about possible redirection in the breadth and depth of your life.

For some retreatants, meaningful and symbolic activities tend to make the reflection and prayer time more significant. If that is the case for you, such prayerful activities are suggested. Use those which open your heart to the waiting God.

The Celtic blessing is a blessing for you, not only to call God's grace upon you, but to give you a sense of Celtic faith. Find a time in your day when you find it to be most useful. Finally, a prayer is offered with which to end your day.

As you undertake this Celtic retreat, God awaits you. It is incumbent that your heart and your soul come to a deep silence so that your yearning for God becomes tangible and so that you can hear the echo of God's longing for you. At the beginning, possibly at the start of each retreat day, quiet yourself with this lovely Celtic prayer of David Adams:

I weave a silence on to my lips,
I weave a silence into my mind,
I weave a silence within my heart.
I close my ears to distractions,
I close my eyes to attractions,
I close my heart to temptations.
Calm me, O Lord, as you stilled the storm.
Still me, O Lord, keep me from harm.
Let all the tumult within me cease.
Enfold me Lord in your peace.

—*The Edge of Glory* (p. 7)

Day one:

The Immanent Presence of God

As a doe longs
for running streams,
so longs my soul
for you, my God.
—Psalm 42:1

Comprehending the reality of God's intimate presence in your everyday life is pivotal to this retreat. It is a grace-dependent understanding which will beckon you to enter into that Holy Presence more deeply. It is the foundation on which subsequent retreat days will be built. So in beginning your retreat, ask for the grace to realize how present God actually is to you. Allow your spirit to sink into this silent Holy Presence.

Immersion into this Mystery is the Spirit's gracious gift to us. Such understanding has not always been so. Christians who today are past mid-life experienced their early formation in faith by learning the questions and answers of the *Baltimore Catechism*. Close to page one came the question, "Where is God?" and the simple answer, "God is everywhere."

By the time the entire catechism was mastered, I for one, believed in an all-holy, all-powerful, all-seeing God who knew my every action and thought—and kept track—and who, on the day of judgment, would call for a strict accounting. Yes, God was glorious in the heavens, but that was an extremely distant place. God was remote from me. I missed the wonderful implication of "God is everywhere"—and therefore intimate. That realization came many graces later.

Those of us who are American women or men religious with pre-Vatican formation probably had an additional barrier. We were taught about a dual world divided into good and evil, holy and profane. The world of prayer was getting at the holy; the active world of play or work, even ministry, was secular. One needed to hurry to prayer in order to find God. We were encouraged to make efforts to "be in the presence of God" while busy with ordinary life. Those efforts were a struggle for me because they seemed to be aimed at forcing the sacred where it didn't fit. My memories of those awkward attempts are of closing my eyes and squeezing my mind in an endeavor to impose God on the moment or the place—to make this far-away God close at hand. Because of their artificiality, these efforts were seldom successful.

But for the Celtic Christians, God was at hand, and their relationship with God was an intimate one. For them, "God [was] the most immediate reality in their lives."[1] These were men and women who grasped the true significance of the incarnation, the full reality of a God who became truly human, like us in all things but sin. Perhaps such understanding was enabled because their pagan ancestors held a deep reverence for all of nature and embraced it as sacred. A pagan god was always found in every natural dwelling. Truly people of the earth, the Christian Celts, while marveling at the actual incarnation, comprehended both the personal and the far-flung effects of God's taking on human form. They felt the presence of the incarnate God, the Christ, almost physically woven into their lives. They knew him to be alive in the stranger, in the friend, in themselves. They recognized God's indwelling in the beauty and power of creation. God was revealed in the mundane and ordinary, and especially in sacred moments and places.

So because the Celts understood God's presence in and through the created world, for them there was no dualism. Nothing was seen as secular. All was holy, or potentially so. Thus, if all of life is holy, all the pieces which make up the mystery of each of our lives are sacred pieces. Patching them together yields the holy.

Translucent Creation

Celtic culture recognized nature as sacred. They saw God everywhere around them, yet they were not guilty of pantheism. The hills, the sky, the sea, the forests were not God, but their spiritual qualities revealed God and were connected to God. All the world was a theophany, a marvelous revelation of God's goodness, wonder, and inventiveness. In Philip Sheldrake's view, "Nature is like a second revelation," a second sacred book.[7] Indeed, their awe of

21

nature enhanced their appreciation and use of the first sacred book, the Bible, especially the Psalms.

Our Creator has been described as an artist, perhaps suggesting a divine imprint upon creation, as brush strokes are reminiscent of a painter. But the analogy is deeper. A painting or a statue, while surely bearing the identifiable hand of the artist, has an existence distinguishable from him or her. But the wonders which God has set in place and continues to hold in existence throughout the globe and far beyond are not totally separable from their creator, their artist. Rather, they have a kind of sacramentality—they bear God's grace and can put us in touch with God. In close harmony with what Teilhard de Chardin brought to our understanding of the created world, Ian Bradley tells us in *The Celtic Way* that human life and all creation is "charged with the potentializing energy of Christ, ever becoming rather than just being."[3]

The early Celts were quite sensuous. They were people who felt keenly and were highly perceptive, attaining awareness through their senses. The beauty they saw, the sounds they heard, the salt air they tasted led them to a profound awareness of the Creator-God. Their pagan predecessors "were not tempted to follow a tradition of containing their gods in temples, but felt closer to them where they could feel the wind buffeting their faces, and see the flash of white wings against the sky, and smell the sun-warmed bark of trees."[4]

Celtic peoples had a special awe for the great eagle. An eagle in flight has greatly enhanced vision and can focus sharply on distant objects. The Celtic church, in David Adam's words, sought to develop the eye of the eagle:

> They prayed that their eyes might be opened, that all their senses might be made alert to that which was invisible. They prayed that they might have the eagle's eye to see him who comes at all times. . . . They soared to the heights of awareness and saw deeper than many people, for they sought to see with the eye of the eagle.[5]

Thomas Merton's life of searching endowed him with an eagle's eye. In one of his numerous works he confesses that when in the woods "I am as aware of God as of the sun and clouds and the blue sky and the thin cedar trees." During the days of this retreat, and indeed all life long, let us pray to have such vision— to see with an eagle's eye.

Thin Places

From the Celts, then, we can learn, not so much about the transcendence of God, but about the immanence. God's fire is near at hand. It burns in and around each of us. The Holy is integral to this place, this moment, this encounter, this event. There is no imposition of God on any of these. The Holy One dwells within, comes out of and through them all. "The sense of the presence of God informs daily life and transforms it, so that any moment, any object, any . . . work can become the time and place for an encounter with God."[6]

And yet, the Celts regarded some places as especially sacred and named them "thin places." These are

23

points of connection and are described as membranes separating the spiritual world from the material world. A plant or animal membrane is a pliable and permeable sheet of cells which allows two-way passage of small molecules between or through the cells of the membrane. Thus, a "thin place" connects the seen and unseen worlds and allows the inhabitants of each world momentarily to cross over to the other. For us, then, it is a place where it is possible to touch and be touched by God as well as the angels, the saints, and those who have died.

Celtic lands provide an abundance of water. The islands are surrounded by the sea, and the land abounds with lakes, rivers, wells, and springs. These in turn cause profuse rainfall so that much of the land is exceptionally verdant; green mountains and hills complete the landscape. All of these—water, forests (especially oak), hill, and mountain tops—are represented among the "thin places" of Celtic lands. Why? The pagan Celts found and worshipped their gods in natural settings, frequently connected with water, oak trees, and hilltops.

In Ireland, St. Patrick and the early Christians actually developed Christianity around many of the pagan sites and customs. Saint Brigid, for example, built her Kildare monastery near the druidic shrine of the goddess of fire and put the unquenched flame to Christian use as a symbol of the light of the gospel. The women of her community attended the fire for a thousand years and have reassumed that function in modern times. Those on whom the fire shines are at a "thin place."

Other places once sought as "thin," and often so recognized today, are those with a long spiritual history. The monastic islands of Iona, Aran, Skellig

24

Michael, and Lindisfarne are still referred to as "holy islands." The locations of other monastic ruins are also among the especially sacred spots, particularly those associated with a recognized holy person, such as a saint's cell or burial site. Any location associated with Ireland's three major saints, Patrick, Brigid, or Columba, is revered as a "thin place" and still draws pilgrims. The Celts have a strong sense of life beyond death. Consequently the locations where people died and where their bodies were laid are included among "thin places."

Today you will want to pray about your own "thin" places and times. Where and when does God permeate the membrane for you? There are spots and moments which cause all of us to gasp in wonder: a burnt-orange sunset, snow shining on a mountain top, the marvel of music, the roaring waves of a sparkling blue ocean, a communion encounter. But each of you has your own unique and special times and places where the holy has met you at least once and where encounter may seem likely again. Name them. Go again in fact or in spirit to a locale or to an experience where God can shine through for you. In all probability there are places which you have not yet recognized as "thin." In seeking these, recall that God's indwelling in our world and in our lives is neither ostentatious nor flamboyant. Rather, God's presence is subtle and deep. One must pierce the veil and search with the eyes of faith.

Recently, alone and awaiting Mass in a small parish church, I found, for a few precious moments, the holy shining through. But as the choir began to assemble for pre-Mass practice, there was exuberant interchange among them and an amazing level of noisy activity. They seemed unaware that they had entered sacred space. The question seemed obvious: what makes space sacred for one and not another? Or, perhaps, what makes a space sacred at one time but not another? The answer in part may be that one must desire to encounter the holy, deliberately enter into the space with reverence, then endeavor to attend to the presence one seeks or finds. Unless we are deliberate, places with which we are familiar may mask their potential for revelation. We must not overlook the obvious. Because all of life is holy, ordinary events, the daily routine, and familiar associates are holy, despite their continuing to appear ordinary and familiar. Everyday places, moments and encounters with others contain and offer to us the intimate God of love. Let us engage our eagle's eye to see below the surface and to see that God is there. Then let us desire, enter, and attend the Holy Presence.

Would-be Olympians, in their training, are told that those before them who have medalled in an Olympic event have excelled in "focus, determination, and commitment." The aspirants are convinced that without the same they will never achieve their goal. There seems to be a strong analogy for us. In our quest for the holy, our ongoing desire for encountering God translates into "commitment"; our entering the moment or the place in readiness and reverence equates with "determination"; and our efforts at attention to God's presence can be expressed as "focus."

In the Stranger's Guise

The presence of Christ in our workaday lives is an ongoing event growing out of the actuality of the incarnation. The marvel of salvation is not solely an historic event. Day to day we need to be immersed in the wondrous reality of the incarnation. In his introduction to *The Edge of Glory*, David Adam says it this way:

> The history of salvation and incarnation has to become our personal history. The Celtic way of ever inviting God into their activities and seeking to become aware of him in everyday events is the most natural way of achieving this. . . . Like the Celtic patterns on stones and in the illuminated gospels, Christ moves in and out, over and under. We are encircled by him; encompassed by his presence and love. This is not something we create. It is a reality to become aware of, a glory that is ours but that we so often miss.[7]

In God's ultimate creation, men and women were gifted with a unique capacity for the indwelling of their creator. There is no surer divine presence than in the human spirit, yet our limits and frailty can make opaque the reality of that sacred indwelling. We know this to be true of ourselves. Intellectually, I can subscribe to the wonder of my being a vessel of God, but my heart can be less sure. There is an ever-present need to grow in that conviction. This applies not only to ourselves but to our view of others as well. Each of us knows good women and men who, for us, are easily transparent to God within. But it can be far easier to recognize God in one who is obviously holy, or in the beauty and power of nature, than to perceive that divine light in the eyes of one who is uninteresting, irritating, angry, or dirty—a stranger to us. We can be sure that the contemporaries of Jesus of Nazareth saw no halo nor divine glow. The face of Christ was a human face. Only deep faith saw beyond it. Now, and ever since, in every human face the face of Christ awaits recognition.

Actual involvement in ministry to our sisters and brothers can open our eyes and lead us into a deeper appreciation of God incarnate among us. A familiar verse illustrates this lesson.

> I sought my God
> My God I could not see.
> I sought my soul
> My soul eluded me.
> I sought my brother
> And I found all three.

The Word-made-flesh gave us the same assurance. "In so far as you did this to one of the least of these, you did it to me" (Mt 25:40).

Celtic Christians treasured the sacramental understanding of "Christ in friend and stranger." It constituted the basis for their hallmark of hospitality. They had a keen awareness that in their treatment of any stranger lay the measure of their treatment of Christ. When we consider the monastic cities we shall discover the extent to which this trait was operational. Monastic space was a safe haven for every stranger. Guests were housed and fed and the ill were cared for. The monastic sense of outreach and mission was keen. The gospel was carried to the uninstructed, and care for the poor and needy was prominent. In the "cry of the poor" they heard the call of Christ.

Many monasteries were founded because of the compelling burden of the gospel and its irresistible call to serve others.

Their bearing the gospel and carrying out its demands was, as ours must be, part of the search for God. "The Celtic Christians did not so much seek to bring Christ as to discover him; not to possess him, but to see him in 'friend and stranger'; to liberate the Christ who is already there in all his riches."[8]

So the presence of Christ in the men and women in our lives is a sacramental presence waiting to be discovered. In opening our hearts to another, the great Other enters. Let us look for opportunities to partake of this sacrament.

The Iona Community offers their Celtic Rune of Hospitality for our pondering:

I saw a stranger at yestere'en.
I put food in the eating place,
drink in the drinking place,
music in the listening place,
and in the sacred name of the Triune.
He blessed myself and my house,
my cattle and my dear ones,
and the lark said in her song
often, often, often
goes the Christ in the stranger's guise.

Who are the Christ-bearing strangers in our lives?

Suggested Scripture for Prayer

(Use one or several as you find they initiate prayer. Or choose favorite passages of your own.)

John 1:1-18	The incarnate Word
Luke 1:39-45	The visitation
Luke 24:13-35	The road to Emmaus
Matthew 11:25-27	The good news revealed to the simple
Matthew 25:31-46	The last judgment
Psalm 8	The beauty of creation
Psalm 42	Longing for God
Exodus 3:1-6	The burning bush

Thoughts for Reflection and Prayer

1. Have I "an eagle's eye" when in the beauty of creation or during an ordinary day?
2. Where are my "thin places"? Let your heart visit one or two in search of God.
3. How do I experience "the Word made flesh" in the stranger? How do I fail?

Prayerful Activities

1. Compose a prayer in which you express: your desire for God's immanent presence, your deliberate effort to enter that presence, your attention to being in the Holy Presence. Pray it often during these days of retreat.

30

2. List the special "thin places" where you have encountered God. Keep the list in a book you use often and add to it as you discover new places.

3. Spend some time in a quiet, pleasant outdoor setting. With the "eyes of the eagle," enter the place and recognize God's presence in various pieces of his world.

4. Then place yourself in a spot of less obvious beauty where people are present. Repeat the effort. What lessons are here for you?

5. At some point during the retreat days select a small memento (e.g., stone, flower, snapshot, sketch) of a God-encountering place. When you return home place the memento where it will serve as a sacramental reminder of how near at hand God is.

Celtic Blessing

Bless to me, O God,
Each thing mine eye sees;
Bless to me, O God,
Each sound mine ear hears;
Bless to me, O God,
Each odor that goes to my nostrils;
Bless to me, O God,
Each taste that goes to my lips,
Each note that goes to my song,
Each ray that guides my way,
Each thing that I pursue,
Each lure that tempts my will,
The zeal that seeks my living soul,

31

The Three that seek my heart,
The zeal that seeks my living soul,
The Three that seek my heart.

—*Carmina Gadelica* (Vol. III, p. 33)

Prayer at the Close of Day One

Great God of Life, I have been surrounded and engulfed by you on this day of grace. You have made me aware of your presence in "thin" moments and places. (Name them.) Just as the deer senses the proximity of water and is drawn to that for which it is yearning, so you have allowed me to thirst for you and to find you very close to me. My heart thanks you and begs for the "eye of the eagle" so that I may see you everywhere. Amen.

Day two:

Presence of the Unseen World

I heard the sound of an immense number
of angels gathered round the throne and
the animals and the elders. . . . Then I
heard all the living things in creation—ev-
erything that lives in the air, and on the
ground, and under the ground, and in the
sea, crying, "To the One who is sitting on
the throne and to the Lamb, be all praise
. . . for ever and ever."
                        —Revelation 5:11, 13

The world revealed God's presence to Celtic
Christians in a thousand ways. The visible world of
creation was not cut off from the invisible world, and
the divine was present in both realms. God's presence
in creation was understood as a sacramental presence. This presence, while genuine, is not observable
with the senses. Yet everything they saw, heard,
touched, tasted, or smelled could connect them to
God, who truly dwells in both worlds. And if this was
true of the presence of the Trinity (or the Sacred
Three, as they said), it was then also true of an un-
fathomable numbers of spirits, both good and evil.
Just as "God is everywhere," so the Celts, with their
strong sense of the supernatural, encountered spirits

everywhere and linked them with all aspects of life. Celtic spirituality is founded on this intense sense and pervasion of Presence and presences.

Often we, in our sophisticated Western world, tend to be somewhat skeptical about supernatural things and events for which scientific evidence cannot be offered. It is common for us to reserve judgment until verifiable facts can be established. Although the use of the scientific method is often appropriate and necessary, this retreat time provides an opportunity to question whether all reality must be substantiated in order to be true. The answer may well deepen our faith life.

We as Christians are called to live in a realm of faith—to be at home with mystery. Does not that gift of faith bring us to believe what we cannot always prove? Paul expressed his concurrence in his letter to the Hebrews: "Only faith can . . . prove the existence of the realities that at present remain unseen" (Heb 11:1). God is the primary mystery whose very existence cannot be subjected to actual proof in the scientific sense. Much of what we know of God comes by revelation—hardly available for microscopic scrutiny. What Christ taught about the Holy Three we accept, not because of evidence but because of faith. Our own experience of God is situated in our hearts and souls, not our heads.

In reviewing the most precious parts of our lives, we discover that we are habitually in the sphere of mystery and the unexplainable. God in human form? in bread and wine? dying for us? impregnating death with life? enabling the blind to see, the crippled to dance? Conviction that this sphere is real requires a kind of perception based not on physical evidence, but on belief in an unseen world. Perception of this sort, according to Noel Dermot O'Donoghue, "reveals a hidden world distinct from both the world of everyday observation and from that opened up by way of rational and reasonable thinking and contemplation."[9]

In his remarkable book, *The Mountain Behind the Mountain*, Father O'Donoghue, a native of Kerry in southwest Ireland, argues that people of Celtic origin have much to teach us about ways of knowing. The approach most familiar to us has to do with attaining factual knowledge. We perceive, or come to awareness, through the use of our physical senses. We see, we hear, we touch, what exists outside and independent of our mind, yet our mind is able to come to comprehension. But humans are capable of another degree of perception whereby our intellect attains awareness or understanding concerning matters beyond the sphere of physical appraisal.

O'Donoghue points toward our power of imagination, by which we conceive something not present to the senses. On one level we use imagination to create the imaginary, which is fictive and exists only in the mind. But imagination can reveal another aspect of reality. It can extend beyond the world of ordinary perception and introduce us to "a world waiting to be found, that does not impose or force itself on us, a world that is at the very center of physical creation as it comes forth from the source." O'Donoghue refers to this world as imaginal, a world which truly exists, but is to be revealed by inner perception rather than by observation. It is a delicate world not subject to our constraints. This is the world where dwell angels, saints, and the living dead. To enter it, he notes, we are "beckoned across the threshold of a sanctuary where we must put off our shoes and tread very gently indeed." In so doing we journey on a road which G. K. Chesterton knew, " . . . a road from the eye to the heart that does not go through the intellect."

Thus, beyond its creative use, imagination is a powerful gift whereby our Creator-God allows invisible reality to be revealed. How so?

> To the senses it says: listen to the Presence, feel it, touch it, breathe it in. To the intellect it says: open up beyond the heavy material world to a Presence and presences that refuse to be controlled by our limiting categories, a Presence that you are longing to encounter and affirm, for it enriches and completes the meaning, the rationale, of creation.[10]

Again, we are being invited to see with an eagle's eye.

Angels and Saints

In the Celtic view, the concealed world of angels and saints was a normal component of creation. The concealment of these creatures made them no less real. In fact, these creatures were considered to be more real because they were not limited by time and place. And so these spiritual individuals were the Celts' life companions.

Throughout their daily routine, Celtic believers acknowledged the presence and sought the aid of the angels and saints of heaven. Rich, poetic prayers were intermingled with their mundane duties. These exchanges were as natural as conversations over tea. In the last four decades of the nineteenth century, Alexander Carmichael went among the people of the Outer Hebrides of Scotland, collected many of these ancient prayers, and published them in the *Carmina Gadelica*. Most of their prayers were dedicated to the prosaic activities of life—sleeping, rising, dressing, kindling and banking the fire, milking the cow, sowing, or harvesting crops. Unseen presences were witnesses to it all, and in true friendship their involvement was sought. A few snippets will serve as examples:

> I will build the hearth
> As Mary would build it.
> * * *
>
> I will kindle my fire this morning
> In the presence of the holy angels of heaven.
> * * *
>
> Come, Mary, and milk my cow,
> Come, [Brigid], and encompass her,
> Come, Columba, the benign,
> And twine thine arms around my cow.
> * * *
>
> Come thou Mary, Mother mild,
> Hasten the butter on the cream.
> See thou Paul and John and Jesus
> Waiting the gracious butter yonder.

And, we are told, persons greeted one another with "God be with ye this day." The plural 'ye' implied that the individual's angel was in his or her company.

While angels and saints could be encountered anywhere and at any time, there were, as we have seen, certain "thin places" where encounter was more likely. While all of nature was regarded, in Philip Sheldrake's term, as a "doorway to the sacred," some locales were more spiritually potent. Among them were transitional places at the edges, boundaries where, for example, the forest met the plain, the water met the land, one county met another. In the case of angels and saints, the edge was sometimes found on the tops of hills, where earth seemed to be contiguous with heaven. But whether the mingling of the earth's seen and unseen citizens occurred in ordinary or in special ways, the aura was one of delicacy and awe. The presence of God's friends and courtiers could not be separated from the Holy Presence, the King of Creation.

And what about our own rapport with angels and saints? Are our conversations with them more "long distance" than intimate and personal? Could we be enriched by deepening our awareness of their inclusion in our world and relating with them as members of God's family? Just as we now have true human friends who reveal God to us, who better than those living in companionship with the Holy One to give us a glimpse? These are the very ones with whom we join at every eucharist to sing, "Holy, Holy, Holy Lord, God of Hosts." Ought we not to seek their friendship?

Our times of prayer today offer the ambiance wherein, if need be, we can lessen our skepticism and intensify our desire to enter this hidden and holy world. Praying with both the Old and New Testament, we can sharpen our appreciation of these companions who function on God's behalf and personify God's provident care and concern for us. The scriptures tell us of holy envoys seen and heard in human form and who communicate God's message, who protect, rescue, strengthen, and guide. They serve as prayer-leaders, companions, comforters, and even match-makers. You may wish to spend the day with the lovely book of Tobit, within which Raphael carries out many of these functions. Or revisit more familiar stories in the gospels such as the annunciation to Mary, the birth of Christ, the flight into Egypt, the agony in Gethsemane, or the resurrection of Jesus. A non-scriptural way of prayer for you could be to consciously spend the day in the company of a favorite saint. Let us listen and learn.

The Living Dead

In an impressive manner some of the living dead are part of our personal world. In all probability you have sensed the after-death presence of someone you have loved deeply. It is reassuring to know that those with whom we have shared life and those especially dear to us are present in the imaginal world to which we have access. What has already been said of angels and saints is true of the living dead as well, for they are among those living in the presence of God. We treat them separately here because the Celts thought of them in a distinct category, and also so as to highlight a truth we already know.

Long before Patrick arrived in Ireland, the Celts believed in life beyond death. In pagan times the Druids taught their own doctrine of immortality, that at death a soul went to a new and better world. Druidic doctrine also proffered the possibility for the souls in the other world to cross over to this world. Thus, in its time, the church's teaching on immortality and resurrection was easily clarified and accepted.

Their mystical sense of thinness led the Celts to a keen cognizance of their closeness to the dead and an ease in dealing with death. The place associated with the life or burial of one they loved was honored as a connecting point. They considered the spot to be holy and a particularly efficacious location for the saint's continuing prayer and influence. Their understanding of the doctrine of the communion of saints, which we profess, was a vibrant one:

> For the Celtic Church it was a very thin line that divides the church triumphant from us on earth. Those who witnessed before us and are received up in glory are very much alive. They are not men and women of the past, but sons and daughters of God, who are alive now and in the fullness of eternal life. The communion of saints is a reality to be experienced.[11]

For both the Celts and us, one implication of this belief is that the holy dead are a living part of the church on earth and therefore an active force in our lives. A second implication concerns the concept of time. For Celtic people the present time contains actual components of the past as well as of the future.

Memory may also connect us with the imaginal world, for our remembering of those in eternity enhances their presence. The past becomes the present. This should not be such a strange thought when we recall the marvel of the eucharist. What we and people across the span of time do "in memory of" Jesus brings that historic moment to every now.

Like the angels and saints, the living dead were numbered among the presences whom Celtic people sensed and honored. They are with God, and they are dedicated to bringing us into that Holy Presence. They prefigure the full realization of creation. As attested by Karl Rahner, "In death the relationship which we have with the world is not abolished, but is rather for the first time completed."

Dark Spirits

Celtic Christians lived with a keen awareness of light, beauty, and the basic goodness of God's vast creation. Hope and joy were constant themes in their life of faith. Yet their earthiness and realism, as well as their access to the imaginal world, revealed evil forces and dark spirits as legitimate components of total creation. These were clear enemies who invaded their world and were to be taken seriously. From Christ in the gospels they learned that these adversaries were not to be destroyed in war-like conflict, but rather to be resisted and defended against.

The Holy Three, angels, saints, and the living dead, who surrounded and companioned them, were frequently invoked as the Celts' protectors. They clearly had greater powers than the dark spirits whom they could keep at a safe distance. At least two types of prayers were used, remnants of which survive in the *Carmina Gadelica*. In the best known *lorica*, attributed to Saint Patrick, he binds to himself the strength of the Trinity against the "demon snares of sin." This sort of prayer is also known as the "breast-plate" prayer, the equivalent of the Latin word *lorica*. The thought of using God's armor for protection was also expressed by Saint Paul, who urged the Ephesians to "put on God's armor," to stand their ground with "truth buckled round [their] waist, and integrity for a breastplate . . . carrying the shield of faith . . . to put out the burning arrows of the evil one" (Eph 6:14-16).

The *caim* was another protection prayer, accompanied by a simple ritual. Using the index finger and turning sun-wise, the invoker drew a circle in the air and begged the Trinity and/or the angels and saints to keep that space safe. For instance:

> My Sacred Three
> My fortress be
> Encircling me
> Come and be.
> Surround my hearth and home.

In battling evil forces, asceticism was considered essential. Some was self-imposed as a required ingredient for spiritual health and growth. Much was in accepting the hard and rugged conditions that, for example, the Irish knew on their wind-swept and rocky land—in disease, crop failure, invasion, or subjugation. Even into our own times these good people have been chastened by a history of privation and oppression. They have also been solidified in holiness by keeping their lives in balance with God and all of creation.

In the late twentieth century, demons, like angels, are frequently ignored or regarded with great uncertainty. As we spend this day in the environs of the imaginal world, let us recognize our need for assistance and protection in the presence of dark spirits.

Suggested Scripture for Prayer

(Use one or several as you find they initiate prayer. Or choose favorite passages of your own.)

The Book of Tobit	A story of divine providence
Daniel 10:1-19	Daniel's vision
Psalm 148	A hymn of praise
Ephesians 6:10-20	Grow strong in the Lord
Luke 1:26-38	The annunciation
Luke 2:8-15	The birth of Jesus
Matthew 4:1-11	The temptation
Mark 1:32-39	Jesus cures the sick
Mark 9:14-29	Jesus cures an epileptic boy
Luke 24:1-8	The resurrection

Thoughts for Reflections and Prayer

1. What stops me from bypassing my intellect and allowing my heart to enter the hidden and holy imaginal world?

2. Who are the living dead whose presence continues in my life? How do I know their presence to be real? Do I converse with them?

3. Am I assured that our loving God and the angels and saints are at hand to defend me against dark spirits?

Prayerful Activities

1. When possible, spend quiet time in a cemetery. Use your imagination to reverently cross the threshold into the imaginal world where you can see that those who are buried in the earth are indeed alive. Ask them to assist you with any resistance you may feel.

2. Go to the grave of a dear friend or loved one and enter into conversation. Share with that person some of your deepest desires and ask for his or her advice.

3. Select several additional friends or relatives and invite them to join you for fifteen or twenty minutes. Dip into the sacrament of memory and talk about good experiences you have shared.

4. Write a *caim* which addresses your guardian angel. With your right index finger trace a circle about yourself as you turn right and pray the *caim* for protection.

5. On this, or another, retreat day, ask a favorite saint to spend the day with you. Discuss with that saint the events and graces of the day as they unfold.

Celtic Blessing

The love and affection of heaven be to you,
The love and affection of the saints be to you,
The love and affection of the angels be to you,
The love and affection of the sun be to you,
The love and affection of the moon be to you,
Each day and night of your lives,
To keep you from haters,
to keep you from harmers,
to keep you from oppressors.

—*Carmina Gadelica* (Vol. 111, p. 209)

Prayer at the Close of Day Two

Dear Creator of all that is, you have taught me today that I share the world you made with many more creatures who are unseen, whose height and weight cannot be measured. When I make use of gifts you have given me to enter the invisible world, multitudes of angels, saints, and living dead are present to me. What a splendid avenue for friendships and grace! Enable me to become more comfortable with entering their world and inviting them into mine. As I lie down to sleep this night, may I be surrounded and protected by these loving members of your family. Amen.

47

Day three:

Faith Lived in Community

They are happy who live in your house
singing your praise all day long.
—Psalm 84:4

How good, how delightful it is
for all to live together.
—Psalm 133:1

The Celts seemed to have a natural disposition for community. The kinship they felt with the angels and saints was complemented by their kinship with one another. Perhaps that is why life shared together in and around the monastery became the ordinary way in which Christian life was lived.

In the glory days of Celtic Christianity, the monastery was the dominant institution. Between the sixth and the twelfth centuries in Ireland alone, hundreds of monasteries were established and flourished. Until the mid-twelfth century, when European Cistercians were brought to Ireland to reform monastic structures, most monastic settlements served as cities where religious and laity lived and worshipped as a community, functioning as the local church, that is to say, as a local subunit of the total church.

When Patrick arrived in Ireland, in perhaps 431, he found a primitive and fragmentary form of Christianity. In his thirty years he solidified and organized the church throughout the country, so that by his death he had established several dioceses, with Armagh as his headquarters. Within a generation or two after his death, however, the Roman influence had withered, and monasteries, rather than parishes, had become the basic units of the church, with abbots or abbesses having more sway than bishops.

In relatively recent times many ruins have been, and continue to be, unearthed. As a result, archeologists and other scholars have enriched our understanding of these monastic cities, so different in structure and function from our present-day monasteries and religious foundations. By that understanding we are offered some striking lessons and a challenge to apply them.

Organization and Location

Modern day exposition of monastic ruins indicates the previous existence of many hundreds of monastic sites of great variety, yet with common patterns. Evidence shows a spectrum of arrangements from a few solitary huts to numerous buildings which appear to have housed several thousand monks and lay persons. It would seem that, as the word suggests, a monastery often originated as a cell for one hermit. As others were attracted by the monk's holiness, the group might grow to twelve, mimicking the number of apostles, and eventually expand into a large monastic city. In its fullest development that city housed a variety of persons of similar mind striving by their lives and work to give expression to their faith. Enclosed by a circular boundary wall, the city had an overall plan, even though buildings might be scattered without apparent order. In our terminology the monastic city could be described as a commune, hotel, retreat house, hospital, school, art center, mission headquarters, powerhouse of spiritual energy, and as the local church, corresponding in some ways to the parishes of our own time.

Space surrounded by the outer wall was considered sacred and was honored as a place of sanctuary. The wall was not intended to exclude those beyond it but to designate safe haven and to confine their animals. Within that enclosure were simple structures for work or dwelling, as well as a great deal of ground for raising animals and cultivating crops. An inner, central area was also walled to define the holiest space where at least one church predominated and where there were buildings dedicated to the monastic life itself. Some monastic cities housed "double monasteries" and enclosed a second parallel space containing "the nuns' church" and their dwellings.

Monasteries tracing their inception to a single hermit's cell tended to originate in wild and remote places, often islands. More populated establishments frequently favored sites which combined seclusion with easy access. Three of the largest and most well-known exemplify different types of locales. Clonmacnoise was built along the Shannon River where the major routes of Ireland crossed; Armagh was on the highest hilltop in the ecclesiastical capital; Iona dominated a hard-to-reach island in the lower

Hebrides of Scotland. Not surprisingly, the Celts situated many monasteries in locations of uncommon natural beauty. Further, foundations were sometimes built on "thin" sites near sacred groves, wells, or springs. All appear to have been in places where the Holy Presence was palpable.

Each monastic city was independent of others, although there were often historical connections among them as well as commonality of structure and function. Simultaneous with the receding influence of dioceses during the sixth and seventh centuries, some monasteries developed familial ties among themselves. These family-like federations (*paruchia*) increased their prestige and power so that *paruchia* became more influential than the diocese. Loyalty to one's given monastic city was forceful because the Celts were inclined toward a tribal society and to strong family ties, both of which were inherent to their city. These qualities, which contributed to the integrity of a monastic city, also help to explain the soundness of its relationship with sister monasteries as well as its cohesion as a local church, so reliant upon the principles of Christian community.

Local Church

The Celts' sense of individual persons and their ease with one another was, surely, another aspect of what appeared to be an effortless reach into the unseen world, about which we prayed yesterday. The communion of saints involves all of those now living on earth and the living dead who once walked the same earth and who continue to be present to us. The local church, the monastic city, was the scene for much of this interaction between those now alive and the living dead, but also for interactions among the living.

In their heyday monastic cities embraced a large proportion of the population on the island of Ireland. Including all classes of society, life was remarkably well balanced. What distinguished it was its being grounded and centered in faith. Membership in the church was a driving force and permeated the spiritual quest as well as all the mundane activities associated with work or pleasure. Life was both humanly satisfying and sanctifying.

These people seem to have achieved the wholeness so craved in the late twentieth century. It is this integration of their Christian lives, and their utter authenticity, which should entice our pondering today. They were the church of their day, and they were wonderfully human. As scholars describe this version of church, the images may well provoke our envy. The monastic environment was non-violent and a ready haven for travelers and for those in need; it was permeated with spiritual energy and invigorating worship; men and women, lay, religious, and clergy functioned collaboratively so that the resulting community was non-hierarchical; the gifts and presence of women were recognized and honored; emphasis was not on ordination or vows, but on personal holiness.

This was the church in action, and its missionary outreach focused on the poor and insignificant. This was a place of culture where wisdom was highly valued, as were education, art, music, and poetry. We may legitimately bemoan that this model of local church does not exist today, but we would do better to emulate whatever we are able. You are part of a local church, whether it be a parish or another version of community. What can you contribute to its enlivenment?

In this Celtic world women were regarded as equal. They were electable for leadership roles, including that of abbess of a monastery of both men and women. Writings attest to the respect accorded to such abbesses as Brigid, Hilda, and Ita and to their pervasive influence in the church of their day. A reverent and wholesome attitude toward human nature put women and men at ease regarding sexuality and their relationship with each other. This wholesome attitude enhanced the attraction of Christian life in monastic cities.

Vowed religious seemed to feel a special obligation to achieve balanced living by periodic withdrawal from regular monastic activity. Places separate from the enclosed monastery allowed their intensified seclusion, prayer, and asceticism. Evidence of such cells, caves, or oratories can still be viewed today, for example, at Glendalough or on Iona. Lay members, as well, apparently sensed a call for some degree of occasional solitude.

Perhaps the marvel is not that such centers of vibrant, integrated Christian life are not common today, but rather that they survived over a span of six hundred years. With the eighth-century arrival of the Vikings there began a long period when monasteries were repeatedly raided, plundered, and burned. To cite a single example, surviving documents indicate that Clonmacnoise was ravaged at least eight times and burned on thirteen occasions. Not a single monastic city seems to have escaped Viking destruction. Yet many monasteries survived multiple tragedies and rebuilt, only to be available for the twelfth-century onslaught of the Normans and ultimately the English. The tenacity of the men and women of Celtic monastic settlements under severe attack speaks strongly of the intensity of their lived faith. In some of today's quiet time, let us look for ways to measure how intensely our actions and attitudes are blended with and bolstered by our faith.

Solitude and Community

The flourishing and longevity of monastery-based gatherings of Christians bespeaks the Celts' comprehension of community juxtaposed with solitude. Esther de Waal, herself a Welsh Celt, has a keen understanding of this balance and refers to it in one of her books by quoting Abbot John Eudes Bamberger:

> Without solitude there can be no real people. The more you discover what a person is, and experience what a human relationship requires in order to remain profound, fruitful and a source of growth and development, the more you discover that you are alone, and thus the measure of your solitude is the measure of your capacity for communion.[12]

Ester de Waal has clearly absorbed the lesson that inner depth determines one's ability to prosper and contribute in community. Unless one is able to thrive when living with oneself, there is little hope for a rich life in community. The reverse is also true. Unless one is selfless enough to live well with others, she or he will be miserable when spending extended time alone. This dual ability for living correlates with one's spiritual solidity and human maturity—a topic we might profitably bring to prayer today.

Celtic monasteries were based upon those of the east, notably Egypt and Syria. The desert fathers, Antony and Paul, were also claimed by the Celts and often honored by portrayal on their high crosses and in other art forms. It is to this connection that the Celts' strong ascetic tendencies are attributable. Celtic lands lack deserts, but the equivalent isolation and hardship were found in such places as wildernesses, rocky heights, and islands. Hermitages were numerous, and the solitary life was considered an ascetic obligation at some time or times, especially for the vowed members of the community. Judging from the lives of Celtic saints, this solitude yielded not only a more intense love for God but also an enhanced love for their brothers and sisters. They knew what Kathleen Norris, in our own day, has mastered: "The desert of deprivation and solitude has always been the spring of self-giving love."[13]

Along with periodic seclusion, the Celtic model, based on eastern monasticism, stressed the communal dimension of religious living. It was an aspect easily adopted. Michael Mitton offers three reasons why. Pre-Christian Celtic society was community-based and -minded, exhibiting a great concern for the needs and cares of one another. Secondly, the Celtic church derived great inspiration from the desert fathers and mothers who lived and witnessed within community. Finally, love for the Trinity was preeminent among Celtic Christians.[14] As pointed out by de Waal, "A God who is Trinity in unity challenges self-centered isolation and points instead to fellowship."[15]

Celtic communities emphasized personal holiness and relationships. The bishops, for example, did not function as authorities, but were active members of the community. They respected its abbatial authority and ministered directly to its people. Any hierarchical organization was absent. It was a community of equals. Each one within the community was responsible to another known as an *anamchara*, or "soul friend." Both lay and religious, soul friends were a distinctive feature of the Celtic church. The principal criterion for selecting a man or woman was personal holiness. The soul friend served as one's confidant, conscience, and guru—not unlike a spiritual director.

With their focus on the quest for God, monastic communities were unworldly, conspicuously poor, and simple. Such qualities do not foster exclusivity. These places nourished genuine concern, member for member and for anyone in human need. Would not sharpening our own capacity for solitude and for community lead us closer to the God for whom we hunger, and to those waiting to reveal that God to us?

Centers for Learning

The Celts of old (and of today) had a decided love of words. They employed those words with artistry in poetry, prayer, song, and stories. Their storytelling helped them enter the world of mystery and wonder, and it was a vital part of their learning experience. Celtic society clearly valued education, and it was an essential component in the life of monastic communities. As it matured, the city itself became the repository of hand-crafted books, thus perpetuating literary classics and especially the Old and New Testaments. Copying and illuminating sacred scripture became the gift and the province of Celtic monasteries at their height. Yet the appeal to the Celtic people themselves was widespread, for they naturally identified with biblical stories, insight, and imagery. Their spirits resonated with the metaphors of nature and the mystical entry into the unseen world.

Scholars, including those from Europe, who came to the monasteries to pursue learning and culture, found a ready welcome. In a strange twist of fate it was there that, during Europe's Dark Ages, intellectual and artistic treasures were preserved and eventually shared again on the continent.

Sense of Mission

Celtic monks had a compulsion to share the joy of their consciousness of the Holy Three and of God's creation. The gospel dictum of mission allowed such sharing, and they seemed possessed by that call. They were ideal missionaries, respecting the culture of those they served. "For them, evangelism was more a matter of liberating and releasing the divine spark which was already there in every person than of imposing a new external creed."[16]

Within their passionate style of evangelization was a sensitivity to the human dignity of those they

58

encountered. Despite their feeling that it was not a long stretch from the naturally good beliefs of their pagan counterparts to Christian faith, they respected the responses of those who resisted. Ultimately, missionary efforts were viewed as the Holy Spirit's domain, so despite the intensity of their work, the results were accepted with humility and abandonment.

God-seekers who came to the city were welcomed, taught, and cared for as a natural part of the activities in a center of learning. Because a high priority was placed on concern for the poor, special and gentle efforts were directed toward them. The simple lifestyle of a monastic community facilitated communication with the poor and often unlearned. However, evangelizing the learned was no less important. No effort seemed excessive in either case. As we shall see later, missionary journeys of remarkable distances and hardships were a normal pattern of monastic life. They sometimes served to further one's own quest for the Holy One and always to carry God to others.

Today's prayer time provides the possibility of an honest look at what propels your Christian life and ministry. How much passion have you to find God in those you serve and to liberate "the divine spark"? Does your amazement at God's love drive you to widen others' experience of the good news? Do you find that as your years of service accumulate, there is less of yourself and an increased wonder at God's presence and action in what you do? Affirmative answers are a measure of grace in your life. I suspect that all of us have found ourselves capable of some self-deception, even self-seeking, under the guise of unselfish service. Beneath a noble surface it is possible to chase personal success, recognition, and satisfaction. We need the self-knowledge born of simple honesty.

Perhaps the remedy lies in something we prayed about the first day—an ever deepening sensitivity to the Holy Presence in and around us and waiting to be unearthed in others. May that be our focal point so that in our efforts to bring God to others, we ourselves may find the Holy One in those to whom we go.

Suggested Scripture for Prayer

(Use one or several as you find they initiate prayer. Or choose favorite passages of your own.)

Luke 9:28-36	The transfiguration
Luke 22:39-46	The agony in the garden
Matthew 14:13-21	The multiplication of the loaves
Acts 2:42-47	The early Christian community
1 John 4:7-12	Love one another
Ephesians 3:14-21	Paul's prayer
Romans 8:1-11	The life of the spirit

Thoughts for Reflection and Prayer

1. Think of facets of your local church in need of nourishment. What insights and gifts have you to offer? How can you contribute to improvement at the local level?

2. When and where are you in prayerful solitude? How does it enrich your life in
   community? Why should community lead
   you again to solitude?
3. As each committed Christian must, are you
   striving to minister selflessly and with passion, and to release the divine spark?

Prayerful Activities

1. List one or more communities of which you
   are an ongoing part. For each consider:

   How does faith manifest itself?

   How does it affect your dealings with each
   other?

   Are there ways in which your faith can be
   more effective in the functioning of the
   group?

   What can you do to bring about more ma-
   ture relationships?

   Draft a few resolutions accordingly.
2. Spend time today in a place of physical solitude. While there, pray about your own
   hunger and need for time and space alone
   with God. Then list the names of those who
   compose your primary community and
   pray for them, one by one.
3. Who serves as a "soul friend" for you? As
   part of your prayer today write a letter to that
   person in which you express some grace,
   question, or insight resulting from these days
   of spiritual quest. Invite a response.
4. Gather two or three friends and discuss
   what you can do with and for one another

so that your faith can truly be a fire which affects some portion of your world.

5. Select a book which you anticipate may challenge you to grow in faith. Give yourself a deadline for reading it. Might you meet with friends to discuss it?

Celtic Blessing

Bless, O God, the household,
According as Jesus said;
Bless, O God, the family,
As becomes us to offer it.
Bless, O God, the house,
Bless, O God, the fire,
Bless, O God, the hearth;
Be Thyself our stay.
May the Being of life bless,
May the Christ of love bless,
May the Spirit Holy bless
Each one and all,
Every one and all.

— *Carmina Gadelica* (Vol. III, p. 355)

Prayer at the Close of Day Three

O Sacred Three, you who are life, give life, sustain life, teach me what life-giving community requires of me. Help me to ground my relationships in you and to burn with the desire to share the faith. Together with those who gift my life, may we continue to discover faith and to call one another to both deepen and make active that in which we believe. Guide us to form a vital church and to live our daily lives as Christians in love with you and with all our brothers and sisters. Amen.

Oay foUR:

The Expression of Faith

Let them dance in praise of God's name,
playing on strings and drums!
For Yahweh has been kind to his people,
conferring victory on us who are weak.
—Psalm 149:3, 4

Deeply felt love requires expression. A young man gives gifts to his fiancée. A child draws a picture for her mother. A woman prepares a meal for dear friends. Each act gives shape to love. So, too, the Celts. Just as their sense of God's presence and love compelled them to mission, it led them to artistic expression using metal, wood, stone, paint, words, and music. These wholehearted artlovers found countless ways to utilize art in expressing their beliefs and their love. The monastic era coincides with the production of the best of Celtic metalwork, manuscripts, and sculpture—all of which attest to their awareness of and yearning for God's immanent presence. Many such expressions have survived the centuries and attest to the depth and beauty of the Celtic people and of their faith. As Ian Bradley notes: "Perhaps the strongest and also the most elusive symbol which our Christian forebears have left us are those endlessly intertwining and interlacing ribbons and ever-twisting spirals which adorn [their art]."[17]

Celtic Design

Intricate Celtic designs are easily recognizable. These characteristic patterns or knots, resulting from spiraling and interweaving lines, are vigorous and symbolic. Some intended meanings are obvious while, with the passage of time, some can only be conjectured. The exceptional interlacing clearly represents the Celtic love of wholeness and implies the interconnectedness of God and all creation. All is holy. Often these extraordinary, twined configurations are stylized representations of revered creatures of the earth symmetrically woven—birds, animals, fruits, foliage.

Some spiral designs pre-date Christianity, such as those carved into the quartz stones at Newgrange at an estimated four thousand years before Christ. Several millennia later, these kinds of pagan symbols are open to interpretation based on what we now know of their culture. It is possible that they signify the circle of protection, the sun-gods, an endless cycle of existence, or creation's non-static process of change. As was always true of the Celts, each of these explanations can be Christianized—and was. In a Christian view, the spirals and interlacing can be read as representing God, without beginning or end, the linkage of things with the Holy, the ongoing process of creation and redemption. Without evident clarity, the symbolism of Celtic design can call us into the great mystery at the heart of Christian faith.

The zenith of Irish achievement in metalwork, manuscript illustration, and stone sculpture was coincident with the six centuries during which Celtic monasteries were thriving. All three art forms employed the symbolic Celtic designs, and items from all three media remain for twentieth century admiration. Some of the most remarkable pieces of metalwork are among the treasures in Dublin's National Museum: the Tara Brooch (seventh-eighth century), the Ardagh Chalice (eighth century), the Derrynaflan Paten (ninth century), St. Patrick's Bell Shrine (eleventh century), the crosiers of the abbots of Lismore (twelfth century), Clonmacnoise (twelfth century) and other monasteries, and the elegant Cross of Cong (twelfth century).

A suggestion for a prayerful pursuit today: depict some facet of your concept of God by tracing a circle and within it sketching an unbroken line which curls back and forth upon itself. This need not be a work of art nor even be shared with anyone. The purpose of the exercise is to initiate you into a physical expression of faith and to symbolize a dimension of inexpressible mystery.

Illuminated Manuscripts

The most intricate of the visual depictions of Celtic belief are their hand-copied books. Books were a necessity in monasteries devoted to learning. In their *scriptoria* Irish monks painstakingly copied Greek classics, Latin literature, their own stories and legends, and of course, the books of scripture, especially the gospels and the psalms. While scripture was required for liturgy and prayer, the very reproduction of parts of the Old and New Testaments was an exercise of contemplation, an avenue for entering into the mystery and wonder of God. Lavish illustrations, in brilliant colors with a generous use of gold, reflect the meditative minds which so carefully produced them. Symbolic designs are profuse, often surrounding words or interspersed among illustrations and portraits. There are occasional imperfections, which, it is said, were deliberate in order to accentuate the limits of the artist in contrast to the perfection of the creator.

An amazing number of these manuscripts are extant; some are over a thousand years old. A description of the most well-known and spectacular one will illustrate something of the marvel of these books. The Book of Kells, the work of many hands, probably originated on the Isle of Iona toward the end of the eighth century. During ninth-century Viking raids, the book seems to have been taken to a sister abbey at Kells for safekeeping and completion. It is now carefully housed and displayed at Trinity College in Dublin.

Intended for use on the altar, this Latin text of the four gospels is considered the most lavishly decorated, with not one of its 680 large folios lacking vivid decoration. By estimation, the skins of 150 calves would have been needed for these vellum pages. A few of these folios have great icon-like portraits of Christ and the evangelists which fill an entire page and are intermingled with richly symbolic designs. The opening words of each gospel are extravagantly illustrated. The motif of Celtic knots recurs again and again, composed of intertwining ribbons, snakes, elongated animals, and human caricatures. Occasional humor punctuates the sacred pages.

For us who rely on imagery to deal with mystery, some understanding of Celtic symbolism may support our imagination—and thus our prayer. The

Book of Kells is replete with hundreds of christolog-ical images. The face of Christ is always portrayed as youthful, radiant, and blond-haired, suggesting di-vinity and unending life. The familiar fish associates the redeemer with the eucharist and with the waters of baptism. It is commonly placed near the face or the name of Christ. Snake ornamentation, represent-ing evil, is combined with references to the passion and crucifixion. More frequently the snake symbol-izes the resurrection, reflecting the Celts' view that shedding its skin renewed its youth. Another metaphor for the resurrection was the lion. This il-lustrates their belief that lion cubs were not born alive but were revived on the third day by the father lion's breathing or roaring on their faces. The lions' link with royalty also transferred to Christ. Peacocks are frequently included to suggest incorruptibility. Eucharistic symbols are pervasive. Hosts, grapes, vines, and chalices are repeatedly worked into an il-lustration. As one views all of this scattered among the calligraphy, there is little doubt how contempla-tive the creation of such a manuscript as this could be. What a wonderful way to give shape to the prayer of one's heart!

What are your symbols for God? A wholesome Trappistine once told me that her major symbol is the moon. She is Belgian, not Celtic, but her rea-son fits: The moon is always there, even when one cannot see it.

High Crosses

The great high crosses are scattered across west Wales, the western isles of Scotland, and in Ireland, where they reached their highest form and where about one hundred survive. Two-thirds of those are well preserved and available to the public. Historian James Roy describes these astonishing works of art as "a Book of Kells in stone . . . an instructional medium of great beauty and obvious sanctity." Others speak of them as "sermons in stone" and "prayer in stone." The descriptor "high" attests to their standing ten to fifteen feet in height, making them a prominent expression of Celtic faith. "Pierced by the sun's rays or silhouetted against an evening sky the high crosses still have an enormous power and presence, standing as silent witnesses to the eternal that is in our midst and pointing from earth to heaven."[18]

Ordinarily of sandstone, these testimonials of faith were formed of three or more separate blocks. A sloping base was understood to portray the sacred mountain of Golgotha. The shaft was the cross itself, the tree of life, the source of all blessing. A most distinctive feature is the ring which encircles the juncture of the vertical and horizontal arms. Theories of its symbolism include: God, the eternal still point of the whole world; the earth itself with the interrelationship of creation and redemption; and the sun, so venerated in Celtic culture. Finally, the capstone seems to represent a special place of prayer such as the temple at Jerusalem, a monastic oratory, or a beehive hut. At the time of their creation, most high crosses are thought to have been brightly painted. Now the colors are long gone, and the crosses stand in stark white contrast with the land and sky.

During the five hundred years of their development, four categories of crosses arose. Early crosses of the eighth and ninth centuries are highly ornamented with Celtic interlace. They mimicked the wooden crosses of the time which were encased in metal and engraved with typical Celtic designs. On the stone, bosses imitated the studs which covered the rivets in the wooden cross. In the early ninth century, transitional crosses began to appear and held panels of scriptural carvings along with the Celtic ornamentation.

Thirty or so of the splendid scripture crosses of the ninth and tenth centuries still exist. These are heavily paneled with biblical scenes depicting salvation and eucharistic themes. On the central portion where the arms intersect, a crucifixion scene adorns one side and the last judgment the other. Interlacing may be used for framing and for edges. These were the teaching crosses around which Christians gathered to listen to salvation history. Even today, as one tries to "read" their well-worn scenes, there is much to stir the soul.

As the invading Vikings began to settle and to become Christians, a Scandinavian influence came into Celtic art. The late high crosses of the eleventh and twelfth centuries bear this influence. More diverse than earlier crosses, they exhibit less ornamentation. The numerous figured panels are absent, and, if interlace is present, it symbolically depicts animals. While a crucifixion scene dominates one side, a figure of an ecclesiastic is portrayed on the other. The latter reflects the beginnings of an hierarchical emphasis in the church.

Clearly the high crosses were a focal point of testimony to Celtic faith. Their placement was at times practical—marking the site of a special event or the entry to the monastic church. But they were also erected at sacred spots and "thin places," such as the burial ground of one considered holy. While knowing something of their purpose or development provides helpful background, these sculptured wonders should primarily feed our spirits. They are marvels intended, in John Sharkey's words, "to stop people in their tracks." They serve as another Celtic form of presence and holiness to be imbibed and absorbed in the depths of one's soul.

Prayers, Poems, and Songs

Gaelic hearts treasure poetry and storytelling along with the words and music which act as their vehicles. Like Jesus, who told stories to deepen understanding, the Celtic church used these vehicles to teach "profound truths in ways that not only fed the mind, but enlightened the spirit and warmed the heart."[19] Here was another mode of expressing the Holy Presence and of invoking God's care.

Poetry and song were often synonymous. Prayers took a lyrical, poetic form. Delight in poetry and music was an intrinsic quality of the Celts. Because these forms bridged the visible with the imaginal worlds they could express the prosaic, the witty, the profound, the mystical. Bards and minstrels, well-trained and highly regarded in Celtic society, would qualify for today's term "professional." These men and women had significant responsibility in what was seen as "an essentially priestly role, in offering up the whole creation to God and standing as intermediaries between this world and the next."[20]

Celtic music seems to have captured the rhythms and sounds of nature. Celts were very much aware of the rhythms of life: work and play, day and night, the changes of the seasons, birth, death, and the aging in between. Work, play, and prayer were accompanied by song in cadences which reflected the rhythm of the activity and touched the Celtic soul. The dramatically difficult times, so much a part of Gaelic history, were times

> when these voices were muted and nobody had the heart to dance; yet in time the deep griefs and calamities of the people found their voice in the lament or *caoine*, by which the voice of pathos took on the force and beauty of that eternal pathos which is the basis of so much of the world's greatest poetry. . . .[21]

One cannot fail to hear the sounds of creation in Celtic music, most prominently the sounds of the island winds and the waves of the sea. Nature's sounds were also caught in the poems from eighth- and ninth-century monasteries. These often came from monks and solitaries who were especially responsive to the beauty and the spiritual quality of the place, and who encountered God in and through their surroundings.

On our second day of retreat we referred to the *Carmina Gadelica*, the collection of Scottish hymns, prayers, and blessings from their oral tradition. The material fills six volumes, so this is a minuscule sampler:

From a hymn of praise:

> There is no bird on the wing,
> There is no star in the sky,
> There is nothing beneath the sun
> But proclaims his goodness.
> Jesu! Jesu! Jesu!
> Jesu! Meet it were to praise him (I, 41).
>   * * *

A mother's blessing:

> The keeping of God upon thee in every pass,
> The shielding of Christ upon thee in every path,
> The bathing of Spirit upon thee in every stream,
> In every land and sea thou goest (III, 246-7).
>   * * *

A journey prayer:

> Bless to me, O God
> The earth beneath my foot,
> Bless to me, O God,
> The path whereon I go (III, 180-1).
>   * * *

From morning to evening:

> Bless, O Christ, my face,
> Let my face bless everything;
> Bless, O Christ, mine eye,
> Let mine eye bless all it sees (III, 267).

Their dancing, too, mirrored God's creation. Characteristic movements

> made the human body in its way a particu-
> larly graceful and subtle musical instrument

74

expressing all human moods, and especially celebrating the rhythms of life in the mutual creativity of feminine and masculine that is, most of all, the basic rhythm of nature at all levels, nature vulnerable to degradation, but profoundly open to resurrection and transformation.[22]

Because these verbal and musical expressions of Celtic faith so attested to their orientation to the God surrounding them and present through creation, they exhibit insight and profundity. The poet Stewart Henderson characterized them as "God thinking aloud." Any true artist must call upon the depth of his or her spirit. With an eagle's eye a writer, musician, or painter must see beneath what is visible. He or she must see the art of life in its ordinary parts and be transformed by that insight. An Irish Sister of Mercy, Aloysius McVeigh, a marvelous artist and a deeply beautiful woman, has said, "The simplest things, the most familiar things, are subjects for art's ennoblement." The ease with which they approached the unseen world may well have enhanced the Celts' artistry. Nevertheless, anyone's ability to give tangible expression to what lies within the spirit marks the maturity of one's spirituality. In some perceptible fashion, let us today give shape to the belief and love so real within our hearts.

Suggested Scripture for Prayer

(Use one or several as you find they initiate prayer. Or choose favorite passages of your own.)

Exodus 35:20-35	The artisans of the sanctuary
Exodus 39:33-43	The tabernacle presented to Moses
2 Samuel 6:1-23	The ark in Jerusalem
Psalm 104:1, 2, 31-35	The glories of creation
Psalm 108:1-6	A musician's prayer
Psalm 150	Praise God with music
Jeremiah 18:1-6	The potter
Ephesians 1:3-23	God, the Creator
1 Peter 1:3-9	Faith tested like gold

Thoughts for Reflection and Prayer

1. Choose a favorite scripture passage and imagine how to illustrate it in a Celtic manuscript.
2. If you do not yet have a symbol for God, pray about it and select one.
3. Spend time studying one of the Celtic designs. How does it speak to you?

Prayerful Activities

1. Write a prayer in poetic prose or verse.
2. Draw a circle. Within it sketch an interlacing line which speaks to you of your concept of God.
3. As love needs to be expressed to be realized, so, too, does faith. Undoubtedly our most frequent expression of faith employs words. Close your eyes and imagine a wordless

symbol or design to represent:
grace
the risen, living Christ
the Spirit of Love
the eucharist

Now sketch one of your designs.

4. Make up a simple melody to fit the words, "You are my God. To you I give my heart." Sing it to yourself throughout the day.

5. Walk to a favorite spot. Search for something which manifests God's love for you. Share your discovery with someone you trust.

Celtic Blessing

God to enfold me,
God to surround me,
God in my speaking,
God in my thinking.
God in my sleeping,
God in my waking,
God in my watching,
God in my hoping.
God in my life,
God in my lips,
God in my soul,
God in my heart.
God in my sufficing,
God in my slumber,
God in mine ever-living soul,
God in mine eternity.

—*Carmina Gadelica* (Vol. III, p. 53)

Prayer at the Close of Day Four

Look upon me this night, O God of Mystery, and bless me. During this day I have tried to enter more deeply into your mystery and to let my imagination and my body give it some shape. Any words or symbols or melodies have been a trivial effort to possess a bit more of you, yet I believe you take delight in my small attempts. They come from a heart in love with you, so let me keep trying and let at least one effort become a sacrament of your presence to me. Amen.

Day Five:

Faith as Journey

"But now, now—it is Yahweh who speaks—
come back to me with all your heart,
fasting, weeping, mourning."
Let your hearts be broken . . .
turn to Yahweh your God again,
for he is all tenderness and compassion. . . .
—Joel 2:12, 13

Pilgrimage and Penance

It is said that Celtic people have wanderlust in their genes. And it may well be true. But, by definition, wandering is an aimless exercise. Simply traveling from place to place does seem to satisfy our need to lessen our boredom with life's routine.

Pilgrimage is on a different plane. While pilgrims do travel, their journey is characterized both by its source and by its purpose. A pilgrimage arises from the desires of one's heart and purports to seek God and the actions of God. True pilgrimage has to do with a change of heart. The outward journey serves to frame an inner journey: a journey of repentance and rebirth; a journey which seeks a deeper faith, greater holiness; a journey in search of God. It is a sacred quest which, using Esther de Waal's expression, must take us into the "inner cave of the heart."

Detailing the history of *Pilgrimage in Ireland*, Peter Harbison recounts it as an unbroken tradition spanning at least fourteen hundred years. The earliest recorded evidence is in the annals of the monastery at Clonmacnoise which account for the death of a pilgrim in 606 A.D. Pilgrimage is common to a number of religions. Over centuries, pilgrims have journeyed to such holy sites as Jerusalem, Mecca, Rome. What are the destinations which drew the Celts?

Recognizing the inseparability of pilgrimage and the Christian demand for penance, the early monks were "ascetic pilgrims" deliberately seeking wild and lonely places out of a sense of their own sinfulness, their need for repentance, and the expectation that God awaited them there. The influence of Eastern desert monastics manifested itself in verdant Celtic lands by the choice of a "desert" of the heart, a place, perhaps in the midst of beauty, which imposed loneliness and physical hardship. These religious were in search of a place which would reveal their God, a "place of special theophany."[23] They viewed themselves as "loved sinners" who chose austerity as a penitential means "to cast oneself upon the mystery of God"[24] and, always, to grow in love. The monks often traveled to other monasteries to visit those considered saintly and to share in their rigor and holiness of life. At other times they sought locations offering extreme solitude and physical difficulty, where uncertainty was its own form of discipline.

Toward the end of their lives, these monastic religious went on a pilgrimage, with no intention of return, in order to seek what they called "the place of one's resurrection." This was their ultimate pursuit of God, for there they awaited death and the eternal theophany. The place was not to be of their choosing, but chosen and revealed by God. Like Abram they heard God's voice, "Leave your country . . . for the land I will show you" (Gn 12:1). Until they were convinced that they were in the land of God's choice they continued to wander and to search for what was to be their final point of passage into the unseen world.

At times, pilgrimage drew these monks to lands beyond their own. A generous response required the utmost austerity, for Celtic peoples were strongly attached to families or communities and to places, particularly when those places were held as sacred. In his pilgrimage which ended on the Island of Iona in 563, Columba exiled himself from his beloved Ireland. The pain of separation was purposefully intensified when he and his companions climbed an Iona hill to make certain that the comfort of seeing their neighboring homeland was no longer possible.

By the late eighth century the phenomenon of monastic pilgrimage abroad had been curtailed. Although their journeys into foreign lands had resulted in conveying the gospel, their presence was not always appreciated by their hosts, especially when large numbers arrived. Such lack of welcome led to encouraging the "pilgrimage of the heart" which could be undertaken in their (and our) own environment. This underscores the importance of the inner journey and adds a spiritual discipline targeted specifically at a change of one's heart.

Whether pilgrimage is actual or interior, each of us needs to understand and to undertake this journey of the soul. The lessons are the same, although physical pilgrimage may make them more obvious. Nonetheless, they apply to every spiritual journey:

- Asceticism, earnestly entered upon, attacks selfishness and enhances the self-giving proper to one hungering for God. Moving toward selflessness leads to grace, to new forms of freedom and to God.
- Pilgrimage strips one of what is familiar and reliable. It breaks our patterns. What a grace this is! In disrupting habits, often mindless, it causes vulnerability and opens one to the new—to God's invading presence—and forces one to rely on that God.
- With very little that is tangible to rely on, everything and everyone becomes a gift, becomes "thinner," making God more recognizable.
- When one fully engages in a pilgrimage, one loses control. The touch of pain and discomfort is inevitable, but so is the touch of the God one seeks.

Pilgrims will attain their goal only if they are already in the company of the God they seek. The power of pilgrimage is in strengthening one's existing attachment to the Holy One. These are profound learnings and compelling reasons to submit ourselves to frequent returns to the desert.

Celtic religious men and women had no monopoly on pilgrimage. The intensity with which lay Christians lived their faith compelled them to seize upon whatever path might lead to God and to lessen the obstacles along the way. Thus, the laity, too, entered into journeys of faith. Modern Celtic lands are peppered with tangible evidence of extensive pilgrimages among them. Lay journeys and destinations differed somewhat from those of the monks, although the effort was still a penitential one and involved a search for special graces and for the holy. More often the journey was of briefer duration. The point to which the laity traveled always had sacred association—the monastery of a holy person, living or deceased (e.g. Glendalough, Clonmacnoise, Aran); a saint's place of birth or death (e.g. Iona, Downpatrick, Lough Gartan); a holy well (e.g. Kildare, Faughert); a particularly rugged location connected with the ascetic practice of a saint (e.g. Crough Patrick, Lough Derg). Large monasteries often kept relics of their holy founders or foundresses and, on occasion, made them available for veneration. These served as additional magnets for lay pilgrims.

The prevalence of pilgrimage in its zenith can be judged from numerous ruins and stone artifacts. Out of their sense of giving hospitality to Christ in the stranger's guise, the monks provided beehive huts or other structures as shelters or hostels for those on sacred journey. Stones were laid as a pilgrims' road which marked the way to a monastery and facilitated traveling. Tall, round stone towers were constructed, the intents of which apparently were multiple. Today some speculate that they served as places of refuge during attacks on the monastic city. Others associate their purposes with pilgrimage. The high tower, visible from a distance, marked the end point of the pilgrimage, giving direction and encouragement to the pilgrims. Its four windows near the top of the round tower faced north, east, south, and west, optimizing both lookout and the sound of bells calling monks and pilgrims to prayer. The entry door is an awkward distance above the ground, perhaps a safety feature, but also possibly for displaying treasured relics without much risk of theft.

Pilgrims, themselves, left evidence of their many journeys. The simplest are, perhaps, the cairns—mounds of piled stones, each of which may have served as a prayer stone or as a sign of successful completion of a pilgrimage to that point. Rudely fashioned crosses, called pilgrims' stones, frequently mark a holy destination. Oratories along the route can also be seen, as can a few ancient sundials used to verify time for the travelers. Two other artifacts associated with pilgrimage are bullaun stones, with hand-hollowed basins to hold healing water, and crosses of arcs, which were flat stones with arcs carved to form a cross of four-point interlace. The latter also seemed to have been indicators of a destination. Some stones exist with only the name or a drawing of a single pilgrim. These artifacts can teach us that there is something sacramental about a tangible memento of a holy journey.

Over the centuries, since the time the earth bore the footprints of so many pilgrims, the trappings for the journey have changed, but the need for pilgrimage endures. Internationally and on our own continent there are holy sites which draw the spiritually hungry. In Celtic lands people still make penitential journeys to places long associated with ascetic practices, and they continue to seek out many of the holy places appropriate to pilgrimage. Why? And why must we, too, be pilgrims?

The answer is inherent in the call to Christian life, in which the cross is central. As spiritual people longing to answer that call, we must live within the paschal mystery. We must enter the cycle of life giving way to death in order that death may give way to life. Like the Christ who taught us this, we must die so as to become new people whose identity is inseparable from God. If we are to become holy, we must become selfless, so that there is room for God to fill us. In *Wind, Sand and Stars*, Antoine de Saint-Exupery says it well: "In anything at all, perfection is finally attained, not when there is no longer anything to add, but when there is no longer anything to take away."

The lessons from the experience of an actual pilgrimage must be transferred to the inner pilgrimage of the heart, a journey we must undertake many times over in our life of discovering God. As our God journeys with us, we need to choose and to submit ourselves to silence, aloneness, loss, ambiguity, helplessness, hunger, prayer. We need to deny our comfortable routine, to forego control, and to enter into uncertainty so that our hearts may expand enough for God's mystery to enter and possess us.

This time of retreat calls us to an inner desert. Let us pray for one another today so that each of us may be gifted with a pilgrim's heart, which is on fire with deep longing for the Holy One, and may be quite willing to enter a lonely desert in order to search.

Clearly, many of our deserts are non-geographical. Some we do not choose. Often it is life's circumstances which offer us the invitation for discipline. The gift of wisdom allows us to see the futility of resisting and struggling against what is inevitable and difficult. Even to grimace and endure is a waste of opportunity. The richness of what the desert holds requires us to enter fully into the journey and so to open ourselves to the revelation of God's presence. In your prayer today ask to identify any loss which might equate to your desert. Is it aging and physical diminishment? Is it to be found in the illness or death of one you love? Is there a broken relationship which also breaks your heart? Is it your struggle in ministry or with the institutional church?

Whatever draws you on this solitary journey beckons you to sharpen your focus on the God of Life and to lessen the self-concern which deters your journey toward holiness. Scripture presents us with graphic desert symbolism. The passage to reach the Promised Land is necessarily routed through the heart of the desert. Whether the journey lasts forty years or forty days, new life lies just beyond. Moreover, we journey in company with the very God we seek.

This fifth day of retreat invites you to spend the day as a pilgrim seeking your heart's desire. Because today's theme pulls together the threads of the previous four days, this day of pilgrimage will lead you to a readiness for tomorrow's day of integration. The very God who so engulfs us creates in us an ascetic sense of our need to trim away whatever detracts us from our deep and singular longing for the Holy One. In the search, we continue to enter the desert where we know God permeates the barrenness. We must do so alone, yet this journey's particular companions are our friends from the imaginal world. And just as the monasteries of the Celts' golden era facilitated the journey of pilgrims, so our communities of faith lend support to us in our travels by their prayer and their provisions. Finally, because authentic faith and love demand tangible evidence, pilgrimage itself is a dynamic which lends dramatic, living witness to what is deep within our hearts. This day of pilgrimage beckons you as a way to give shape to your most profound belief and desire.

Suggested Scripture for Prayer

(Use one or several as you find they initiate prayer. Or choose favorite passages of your own.)

John 12:20-36	The hour has come
Matthew 3:1-12	The preaching of John the Baptist
Luke 4:1-13	Temptation in the desert
Luke 9:51-62	The journey to Jerusalem
Luke 12:22-31	Trust in God's care
Hosea 2:16-21	The call to the wilderness
Romans 6:1-11	The paschal mystery
1 Corinthians 1:17-25	The wisdom of the cross
2 Corinthians 4:7-18	We are earthenware jars

Thoughts for Reflection and Prayer

1. Recall a recent journey to the "desert." What were its lessons? Have you a memento of that journey?
2. When did you enter upon a pilgrimage of the heart? Where did it lead you?
3. How do you render yourself vulnerable and reliant only on the God you seek?

Prayerful Activities

1. Find a spot to serve today as your desert. It might be a place lacking beauty, comfort, light. Go there and pray.

2. Designate this as a day to fast or at least to deprive yourself of some foods which appeal. When at meals, consider: what is the value of what you are doing?

3. In your "desert place" enumerate a half dozen reasons you are in need of God's mercy and grace. Opposite the reasons, indicate how God's forgiving mercy has touched you and, perhaps, ways in which God has lessened your need.

4. Take your list with you when you receive the eucharist. Hold it in your hand and let God's love and hope engulf you. Express your longing for God's presence.

5. Gaze lovingly at a crucifix and ask your Redeemer to reveal to you the need for pilgrimage. Thank him for going into the desert for you.

Celtic Journey Blessing

May God make safe to you each steep,
May God make open to you each pass,
May God make clear to you each road,
And may he take you in the clasp of his own two hands.

—*Carmina Gadelica* (Vol. III, p. 203)

Prayer at the Close of Day Five

God of the Desert, you await me in places I have not yet been. Give my soul the desire to be a pilgrim in search of you and to seek you in places apart. Help me, too, to realize that the desert can be in my heart. Show me ways in which to clear that heart for you. Let me pursue you many times, wherever it takes me, and let me rediscover you, over and over, until I come to the "place of my resurrection." Amen.

Day six:

Vital Living and Commitment

I must fulfill the vows I made you, God;
I shall pay you my thank-offerings,
for you have rescued me from Death
to walk in the presence of God
in the light of the living.
　　　　　　　—Psalm 56:12, 13

We have seen that a Celtic design presents a line which crosses and weaves in an apparently inseparable fashion. Without discernible start or finish, the art symbolizes the integrity of the whole. We know it to suggest that all of God's creation interconnects and is an embodiment of the Creator. That which extends from and reveals the Holy One is itself a holy sacrament. The inescapable conclusion: all creation is holy; all of life is holy. We are called to embrace both fully.

The related etymologies of 'holy' and 'whole' give credence to the Celtic awareness of the synonymity of the concepts. These people comprehended why the totality of creation and life is holy and, in turn, that what constitutes the holy is wholeness, health, unity with the Holy One. If true of inanimate creation, how much more so of the creature in whose form God chose to take flesh?

Because they saw the aggregate, for the Celts there was an absence of boundaries between the secular and the sacrament. The texture of human life was a sacred one. Thus they had a great taste for all of life and fully immersed themselves in it. For these wonderfully sensuous people, the living body enabled them to know and express the fullness of the human experience. To laugh and cry, to sing and dance, to work, to love, to be loved, to sense the Holy Presence, were some of the threads woven to make them fully alive, human, holy. Their zest for life enabled them to balance and to integrate all the pieces and, in so doing, to become authentic human beings. Here was other visible evidence of their faith. They, themselves, became that evidence and lived the whole of the earth-bound portion of their Christian lives with passion. God surely responded to their asking:

> Holy God, make us holy,
> Wholesome God, make us whole,
> Healthy God, make us healthy,
> Holy, Strong One, God Almighty.[25]

Much about which we have prayed in earlier days of our retreat gives depth to understanding how the Celtic Christians of the Middle Ages were whole and holy men and women. Today we will focus on three other manifestations of human authenticity: their simplicity, their relationships, and their openness. It is from within these three qualities that a commitment to living the evangelical counsels of poverty, chastity, and obedience takes shape for religious as well as laity.

Simplicity

Celtic peoples had little taste for power, complication, or material goods. Despite the magnificent intricacy of their works of art, these were rural people who lived in an earthy fashion and also saw beauty in what was plain. The communitarian nature of their monastic cities put emphasis on the fact that the totality of the land and their holdings belonged to all who lived together. John O'Riordain notes that

> there is no word in the Irish language for 'private property' and there is no verb 'to possess.' The term for one's property is *mo chuid*—my portion; the underlying social and legal position being that the wealth of the community was owned by the community and out of that resource each got enough to live on.[26]

Such an arrangement is remarkably parallel to that of religious with a vow of poverty. Therein an individual member receives a share of what belongs to all. But lay Christians, as well as religious, can be instructed by the simple and earth-related lifestyle of these good Celtic people.

Because the beauty and power of natural creation revealed God to them, they viewed nature with awe and wonder. Its sights and sounds led them to poetry and prayer. Like their pagan ancestors who worshipped the earth-goddess, *Anu*, as the source of fertility, Celtic Christians revered the earth as a life-giving mother. This attitude toward and their harmony with the earth was an integral part of their spirituality. And what of us in this time and place? Although there is a twentieth-century resurgence toward honoring the earth, it rises out of decades of disrespectful usage and exploitation. We cannot continue to be part of that injustice if the earth is revelatory of the God whom we seek. This time of retreat is opportune for us to consider ways in which our lifestyle dishonors the sacrament of the earth and, on the other hand, to find some means to repair both our and others' disrespect. We fulfill a priestly role by shouldering an effort to bless our land.

For most of us the environment in which we live is urban and sophisticated. We are pelted with the noise and sensationalism of the various media. We are bombarded with technology-dependent communications. Shallow materialism and consumerism is accepted as a way of modern life. As offered, our American lifestyle is not simple. And our choosing simplicity is not, of itself, a simple choice. The pursuit of simplicity today is ascetic, and Christians need to be at home with that discipline, so crucial for our growth in faith. Narrowing one's attention and involvement facilitates focus on the God in whom we are immersed. By reining in a wide scattering of "things," we are better able to plumb the deeper facets of life. What is simple is also profound.

Take space and time today to ask seriously, "Where and how can I become a more simple person, a less complicated consumer?" Simplicity of life has far-reaching effects. It sharpens our sense of oneness with our human peers. A consciousness that we share the earth necessarily enlarges our world to include other earth-sharers. Interdependence and unbiased inclusivity become bright realities. Our spiritual vision becomes keener—like that of the eagle held in such repute by the Celts. With the eagle's eye we *see*,

96

not just look. In seeing, the eye penetrates the surface and comes to understand essences. So let us join the Quakers in singing, "'Tis a gift to be simple; 'tis a gift to be free," and let us make the song our prayer.

Relationships

Jesus' gospel is rich with example after example of the value and importance in which he held relationships. God in human form loved warmly and was almost unreasonably faithful to his friends. How humane the instances of his heart being "moved to pity": his sadness at the death of Lazarus, his patience with Peter, his compassionate touch of the diseased and disabled, his utter kindness to Mary of Magdala—to name but a few. Celtic Christians took readily to this facet of Christ's teaching and example, no doubt because strong, human relationships were natural to their culture. As unimportant as the trappings of power and possessions were to these people, human relationships were essential to them. Just based upon what is known of their relish for the human experience, one can conclude that kinships, friendships, and communications were of primary concern. And, we recall, these were sensuous men and women who employed their bodies in both the perception and enjoyment of life. Their expressions were warm and affectionate and emanated from the heart of their faith. Intimacy with the triune God who modeled relationship and friendship with others was a constituent of their spirituality. In his book *Wellness: Your Invitation to Full Life*, John Pilch states for our

97

time what could well describe Celtic times: "Spirituality that is not sensuous is not authentic."

The holism of Celtic relations can be easily exemplified. We have already noted their identification of Christ with the stranger. Warm hospitality resulted from that recognition and was offered with deep and holy respect. Honoring the inherent dignity of their neighbors was a given mode of living. The greeting of a visitor in a friend's home often was "God's blessing on the work," accompanied by brief, symbolic participation in that work. Prayers when kindling the morning fire might include "Kindle in my heart within a fire of love of my neighbor," asking that the fire of love shine out "to my foe, to my friend and to my kindred all." Meals were seen as an appropriate celebration of life and as a means of unifying those who dined together—not so different from our appreciation of the eucharistic meal. Finally, a person's unique relationship with a "soul friend" highlighted the spiritual level appropriate between true friends.

Psychologists of more recent centuries would, no doubt, pronounce these Celtic relationships healthy. Their integration of the physical and the spiritual provided for balance and wholesomeness. It continues to be true that love is the yardstick whereby the degree of one's human authenticity can be measured. Moreover, love is the one enduring quality of genuine relationships. And love is the coinage of the kingdom of God.

During this day, as we look at our own relationships, let us attend to how truly they provide insight into our growth in grace. This seems to be the arena in which our humanity is best tested. Whether celibate or married, whether we have parented or not, the richness of our person is determined by our own sense of being loved and by our capacity for loving others. We gain some insight into what it means to be loved by God, and some know-how about loving God, by being the recipient of true human love and by learning to love others without self-interest. Without the warmth of human interaction we cannot grow spiritually. Without this human experience, it is hopeless that our relationship with God will penetrate very deeply into the holy mystery. Without our knowing first true human and then divine love, it would be difficult to move beyond self-love into the self-giving so descriptive of being genuinely human. We need to pray this day about this most basic arena of human experience. What have we learned by being honestly loved by a parent, a sibling, or a friend?

Those of us committed to celibacy must surely understand the special place of human love in our lives. Unless we genuinely love other humans and demonstrate that love warmly, we are not perceived as sincere ministers of a gospel of love, nor can our love for the God revealed in that gospel be in full bloom. Our challenge is to evidence our love with ardor, but without the sexual expression so beautifully appropriate for husband and wife. Married Christians who enter fully into love's physical intimacy enter a sacrament of love and must become its conduits. Let us ask this day that nothing in us will impede the passage of God's love through us to others. Perhaps our prayer ought to be that there be a "thinness" in any encounter between ourselves and another human being.

Openness

Both simplicity and selfless love tend to open our minds and hearts to the penetrating presence of the Sacred Three. And openness itself is a virtue for which we need to strive. Only those who are open are able to receive God's mysterious gift of grace— and are able to recognize that everything is gift. Openness requires that our sense of self be in true perspective. Being open can be equated with humility. A Celtic night prayer seeking greater intimacy with the Holy One asks that God pierce "my eye of blindness." Commenting on this desire to reach and root out the "hidden veins of selfishness and self-conceit," Noel O'Donoghue remarks that our blindness can and must yield to "prayer by which the eye of the heart opens beyond its own conceits to the humble acceptance of a higher light and a higher wisdom."[27] He is suggesting our need to see ourselves with an eagle's eye.

Such openness is a surrender to God's action and God's will in our lives. A radical degree of listening is required so that what we hear is subjected to the light of reality. The Latin word for "obedience" can be translated "to listen." So obedience comes out of radical listening and scrutinizing what we hear in the Spirit of Jesus. Discerning the message in our encounters, in life events, and in prayer is a prelude to knowing what it is God wills for us. It also requires understanding the concept of God's will.

There are some who believe that we "do God's will" only when we "get it right" in making a choice among possible options. Such an approach resides in the stressful premise that for each of us there is a checklist of where we must be and what we must be doing in order to fit into God's plan. This is not the God of the Celts—nor, I hope, of us. Rather, God's plan for us is a large picture and provides for our becoming fully and lovingly human and holy in our own unique circumstances. We learn how best to do that by prayerful openness and listening so as to measure our choices against the standards of the gospel and our own God-given gifts. Whether on a given day we turn to the right or to the left, God waits on the road, but we must choose. We must be sensitive to that presence. This kind of listening is incumbent on all whose lives are a search for the God of love and holiness. For those vowed to obey it takes us far beyond a choice of ministry or submitting to legitimate authority. Listening opens our heart to make room for a divine encounter. The Celts, daily and in every circumstance, spoke prayers like "Blessed be the Holy Will of God," or "'Tis a fine day (or a wet day), thanks be to God." May their saints teach us that all is gift and that everything reveals the God of mystery.

Suggested Scripture for Prayer

(Use one or several as you find they initiate prayer. Or choose favorite passages of your own.)

Deuteronomy 30:15-20 The two ways

Micah 6:8 Act justly, love tenderly, walk humbly

Psalm 139 God's love is everywhere

Isaiah 25:6-10 The messianic banquet

101

Isaiah 49:1, 2, 15-16	"I will never forget you"
Luke 12:13-21	The false security of possessions
Luke 15:11-32	The prodigal son
1 John 4:7-21	Love one another

Thoughts for Reflection and Prayer

1. Examine your responsibility for God's earth. In what practical ways can you respect and bless it? Is there a way you can influence the attitude of others?

2. Are you a typical twentieth-century consumer? What barriers prevent your living more simply? Consider how you can remove at least one such barrier. Can you foresee how simplification can sharpen your ability to *see* rather than look?

3. Think of one of your human relationships which enriches your faith life and facilitates your growth. What is it about this particular interaction which makes it so special? What is the lesson to be learned here?

Prayerful Activities

1. Make yourself a cup of tea, and as you enjoy it sing, either aloud or to yourself, the Quaker hymn, *'Tis a Gift to Be Simple.*

2. As you take a walk, observe evidence of human exploitation of the earth. In what new ways can you honor God's earth? How

102

would they connect you to a more simple style of life?

3. Is there a relationship with a friend or family member in need of repair? Write a letter admitting your share of the blame and asking to meet. You may or may not choose to send the letter. Perhaps a conversation would be better, or, at a minimum, pray for the heart to approach him or her.

4. Imagine you have been asked by a friend to advise her about choosing between two opportunities for ministry. In a letter to your friend, address the question of God's will for her.

Celtic Blessing

The eye of the great God,
The eye of the God of Glory,
The eye of the King of Hosts,
The eye of the King of the Living,
Pouring upon us
At each time and season,
Pouring upon us
Gently and generously.
Glory to thee
Thou glorious sun
Glory to thee thou sun
Face of the God of Life.

—*Carmina Gadelica* (Vol. III, p. 307)

Prayer at the Close of Day Six

Holy God of Wholeness, do bless me this night by steeping me in human authenticity. Narrow my concerns about material things; broaden my love and care for others; deepen my ability to hear clearly and correctly. I beg you to open the eye of my heart so that with an eagle's eye I may penetrate the surface and recognize the foolishness of a cluttered life, the wholesomeness of genuine and mutual love of family and friends, your deepest desires for me. Amen.

Day seven:

Reviewing the Retreat

We last no longer than grass,
no longer than a wild flower do we live,
one gust of wind and we are gone,
never to be seen there again;
yet Yahweh's love for those who fear him
lasts from all eternity and forever.
                              —Psalm 103:15-17

Every good teacher tells you again what she or he has already told you. Educators know that repetition and summary strengthen learning. That principle can also be applied to a retreat. Every sincere retreat is alive with God's grace. A review of those graces can reinforce them and enhance the fruitfulness of these days. These have been days in pursuit of God, along with efforts to correct our course. How has God revealed himself and his love to you? What has God taught you during this graced time? What are you resolved to do differently? Let us take another look, and do so through the lens of God's amazing love for you, using that perspective to integrate the six themes of Celtic spirituality about which we have been praying.

Celtic partiality toward John's gospel and epistles was rooted in his keen penetration into the mystical.

107

In those writings we can discover many of the characteristics of the Celtic spirit, a fact which gives credence to the universal applicability of their approach. Recall that John is symbolized by the eagle, an additional reason for Celtic bias in his favor. So spend some time with John. Let him be your companion today and in the days ahead. Love is his constant theme. Living in love and with love brings us to holiness because "God is love" (1 Jn 4:16) and "everyone who loves is begotten by God and knows God" (1 Jn 4:7).

Review of Day 1

Indeed, the Celts knew God. They grasped the human significance of the incarnation. God was immanent, intimately at hand, both without intermediary and through creation's "thin places," in the stranger, the friend, one's kin, oneself, in every moment, event, and place. Jesus predicted this kind of keen, penetrating vision (an eagle's vision) for his friends: "The world will no longer see me; but you will see me, because I live and you will live" (Jn 14:19). With John the Celts could easily say:

> Something which has existed since the
> beginning,
> that we have heard,
> and we have seen with our own eyes;
> that we have watched
> and touched with our hands;
> the Word, who is life (1 Jn 1:1).

We, too, are gifted with the capacity to see, to hear, to touch this God of love in the sacrament of this very moment and in all the moments of our days. How can we hone that astonishing power?

Review of Day 2

Along with God, creator and passionate lover, we are surrounded by members of God's family who either were never, or are no longer, limited by time and space. Angels, saints, and the living dead, though unseen, made their actual presence known to the Celtic Christians who were so at home with mystery. They are accessible to us as well. Although in actual fact "no one has ever seen God" (1 Jn 4:12), that presence is made manifest in visible ways. In like manner the other unseen presences can be recognized in some visible form, as when Mary of Magdala, seeking her crucified Lord on the first Easter, saw and conversed with "two angels in white sitting where the body of Jesus had been" (Jn 20:12). But in either case, visibility is not the criterion for real presence. It is our belief which lowers the threshold for our entry into the imaginal world. Once there we realize that it takes the mutual love of the entire church, of its every member, for God's love and plan to be complete (1 Jn 4:11, 12). Are we not richly blessed to be an active participant in an interacting circle of divine love? Are there steps I can take to embody in daily life that sense of loving and being loved?

Review of Day 3

While we have that happy fortune of being a vital part of God's total family, until we ultimately join its larger and unseen portion, our daily operations are within the visible church as a member of God's earth family. As John echoes Christ's oft-repeated charge that we "love one another" (Jn 13:34), he reminds us "of the love that the Father has lavished on us" (1 Jn 3:1) and points toward the remarkable holiness awaiting those who seriously enter a life of love. Just as the Celts' monastic cities provided the locus for their faith-grounded lives, so our local situation within the church is the framework for our loving one another and our reaching out to those who do not yet understand the wonder of being loved by the God who made them. We are summoned to be a force within a loving community of faith. How are we responding to that vocation? It is the measure of our genuine care for one another that determines the degree of the life of God within us (1 Jn 4:12). Conversely, our personal love for the God of exorbitant love correlates with our ability to see beyond the surface and to truly love those who come into our lives (1 Jn 4:21).

Achieving this two-pronged love of God and of one another—actually two aspects of a single love—brings us toward the best of our human potential and, of course, gives credibility to our faith. If our mode of daily life flows out of our active and prayerful role in a loving community, we will move toward achieving a local Church not unlike that which the Celtic Christians knew. Within that model we will testify to our belief in non-violence, respect for all life, rich relationships, a collaborative, inclusive model of church, and the importance of ongoing learning and human development. "Love will come to its perfection in us . . . because even in this world we have become as [Jesus] is" (1 Jn 4:17). What is it these retreat days call me to do so as to live my faith in a community and contribute significantly to it?

Review of Day 4

Just as functional faith shapes the way we live together, it also influences how we express our belief and its accompanying love. For the Celtic peoples, unique designs captured on metal, stone, and parchment delved into mystery and reflected it symbolically; words were tooled into the poetry and prayer coming from one's innermost faith; notes were woven into music depicting the songs of the heart. Their friend, John, told them—as he does us—"Our love is not to be just words or mere talk, but something real and active" (1 Jn 3:18). While art is a particularly appropriate medium for delineating belief and love, one's deeds must also leave no doubt about the message. We Christians surely appreciate the unreasonable extent of love proven by the redemption, as well as the truth of Jesus' claim: "One can have no greater love than to lay down his life for his friends" (Jn 15:13).

The extremism of dying on a cross puts us in awe of the Christ "lifted up from the earth" (Jn 12:32). To convince us that we are capable of returning his love, he took dozens of occasions to put human dimensions around his love. One of the most charming and moving was his cooking breakfast on the Galilean shore for seven of his friends (Jn 21:1-14). Six of the seven had failed to stand beside him as he died. Apparently that breach of friendship was not mentioned during this incident. Think about the wonder of the risen Christ building a charcoal fire, cleaning fish, procuring bread, and serving these amazed men. What a wholesome expression of affection! Pieces of ordinary life are also available to us as a means to express our love for our God. How have you done this? Are there new approaches you are determined to take?

Review of Day 5

Among the Celts, a common expression of their love and their need for God was pilgrimage. They could never get enough of God and often sought a deeper presence and a fresh supply of God's grace. We are compelled to do the same, and so pilgrimage into the desert—whether actual or in one's heart—is required of us as well. Such a journey is interlaced with discipline in an effort to concentrate and focus on love and to lessen one's self-love. We do so by leaving the familiar, losing what is ordinarily reliable, and relinquishing control. By choice, we become vulnerable to God and gain new access to the Paschal Mystery, wherein life gives way to death in order to enter new life. Pilgrimage is born of listening to what Jesus told us: "Unless a wheat grain falls on the ground and dies, it remains only a single grain; but if it dies, it yields a rich harvest. Anyone who loves his life loses it; anyone who hates his life in this world will keep it for the eternal life" (Jn 12:24-25). Before you take leave of this retreat, discuss with the God of your heart your plans for meeting on pilgrimage.

Review of Day 6

"For the Father, who is the source of life, has made the Son the source of life" (Jn 5:26). And John's reflection on that thought: "We can be sure that we are in God only when . . . [we are] living the same kind of life as Christ lived" (1 Jn 2:5). When John conveys to us these words of Jesus, he is revealing the secret of healthy and holy living. Celtic followers of the gospel caught these messages, which fit well their concept of the wholeness and holiness of life: their invariable awareness of and affection for God, the Source of Life; their esteem for both their seen and unseen companions; evidencing the primacy of their belief through their work and their manner of living and relating. All of this identified them as Christ's disciples and gave depth and breadth to their lives.

The Christ whom they loved and listened to recognized and honored the fact that one "who is born of the earth is earthly and speaks in an earthly way" (Jn 3:31). His call to live life fully incorporated simple metaphors which helped them not only to absorb the mystical but to connect the spiritual with the earthly. Echoes of the wholesome life of the Celts as simple, open, and grounded in relationships can be recognized in Jesus' metaphoric self-descriptions, and those he accorded to the Father, the Spirit, and to his followers:

"I am the good shepherd . . . and I lay down my life for my sheep" (Jn 10:14-15).

113

"I am the light of the world" (Jn 8:12) ". . .
whoever believes in me need not stay in the
dark any more" (Jn 12:46).

I am "the bread of God . . . [who] gives
life to the world" (Jn 6:33).

"The water that I shall give will turn into
a spring inside . . . welling up to eternal
life" (Jn 4:14).

"My food is to do the will of the one who
sent me" (Jn 4:34).

"I am the bread of life," (Jn 6:35) " . . . anyone who eats this bread will live forever" (Jn
6:51).

"I am the true vine. . . . Every fruitful
branch will be pruned" (Jn 15:1, 2).

"Your sorrow will be turned into joy,"
like the joy of a woman who, in giving
birth, "forgets the suffering" (Jn 16:20-21).

"The Holy Spirit [who is like the blowing
wind (Jn 3:8)] will remind you of all I have
said to you" (Jn 14:26).

These precious words come from a heart afire
with love and compassion for us—the same heart that
utters the astounding sentence, "I call you friends"(Jn
15:15). Think of it! The God of all, by whom every created thing is sustained, to whom the angels bow and
the world is subject, this God calls us friends. Bask in
that happy realization, and while in its aura, think
anew about our being so intimately a part of the earth
and the simplicity to which that calls us. Consider,
too, how that intensity of being loved by God ought
to imprint itself upon our relationship with this Holy
Lover and with other human beings who are equally

loved by their God. Finally, reflect upon the appropriate openness and surrender to Love, who pursues us. In the days ahead you might spend time with John, especially with his first epistle and with the last five chapters of his gospel, to celebrate the graces of these days and to continue exploring and integrating the spiritual way of the Celts. And ask John, the eagle, to help you truly see.

Suggested Scripture for Prayer

(Use one or several as you find they initiate prayer. Or choose favorite passages of your own.)

John 14-18	The last discourses
1 John	Love and faith
Romans 8:31-39	If God is for us, who can be against us?
Psalm 63	Desire for God
Psalm 89	An everlasting covenant
Psalm 104	The glories of creation
1 Corinthians 13:1-13	The greatest gift is love

Thoughts for Reflection and Prayer

1. God's presence in your life is a genuine presence and a consequence of God's incredible and personal love for you. Take a few moments just to acknowledge that reality

2. You are a beloved member of God's family. Converse with one or two unseen members (angels, saints, living dead) about that fact.

3. A group of the visible members of God's family constitutes the community in which you live. Ask God to show you just one area in which you can be a more vital community member. Formulate a resolution in that regard.

Prayerful Activities

1. Write a love letter to God. You may wish to include sentiments and resolutions to which the above reflections led you. Or you may prefer simply to pour out your heart in any way which love compels you.

2. Christ put some of his friends at ease with his risen presence by cooking and serving their breakfast. Make plans for a practical way to express your love for God or for one of his friends.

3. Recognizing your hunger for God should make clear the need for frequent pilgrimage of the heart. Think in terms of the year ahead and plan when and possibly where you will go on pilgrimage.

4. Allow yourself to think freshly about the amazing degree of God's love for you. In the light of that awareness, what new efforts will you make toward living a simpler, more open life marked by warm and genuine relationships? From deep within your heart, write those intentions and place them where you will read them frequently.

5. Put in writing a prayer to close this retreat.

Celtic Blessing

The peace of God, the peace of [all],
The peace of Columba kindly,
The peace of Mary mild, the loving,
The peace of Christ, King of tenderness,
The peace of Christ, King of tenderness,
Be upon each window, upon each door,
Upon each hole that lets in light,
Upon the four corners of my house,
Upon the four corners of my bed,
Upon the four corners of my bed,
Upon each thing my eye takes in,
Upon each thing my mouth takes in,
Upon my body that is of earth
And upon my soul that came from on high.
Upon my body that is of earth
And upon my soul that came from on high.

—*Carmina Gadelica* (Vol. III, p.265)

Recommended Reading

Adam, David. *Cry of the Deer*. (London: Triangle, 1987).

_____. *Eye of the Eagle*. (London: Triangle, 1990).

_____. *The Edge of Glory*. (London: Triangle, 1985).

_____. *Tides and Seasons*. (London: Triangle, 1989).

Bradley, Ian. *The Celtic Way*. (London: Darton, Longman, Todd, 1996).

de Waal, Esther. *God Under My Roof*. (Orleans, MA: Paraclete Press, 1995).

_____. *The Celtic Vision*. (Petersham, MA: St. Bede's Publications, 1988).

_____. *Every Earthly Blessing*. (Ann Arbor, MI: Servant Publications, 1992).

Harbison, Peter. *Pilgrimage in Ireland*. (London: Barrie and Jenkins, 1991).

Mitton, Michael. *The Soul of Celtic Spirituality in the Lives of Its Saints*. (Mystic, CT: Twenty-third Publications, 1996).

O'Donoghue, Noel Dermot. *The Mountain Behind the Mountain*. (Edinburgh: T & T Clark, 1993).

O'Riordain, John J., C.Ss.R.. *The Music of What Happens*. (Winona, MN: St. Mary's Press, 1996).

Roy, James Charles. *The Road Wet, the Wind Close*. (Chester Springs, PA: Dufour Editions, 1986).

Sellner, Edward. *Wisdom of the Celtic Saints*. (Notre Dame, IN: Ave Maria Press, 1993).

Sheldrake, Philip. *Living Between Worlds*. (Boston: Cowley, 1995).

Endnotes

1. Esther de Waal, *The Celtic Vision*, (St. Bede's Publications, 1988), p. 5.
2. Philip Sheldrake, *Living Between Worlds*, (Cowley Publications, 1995), p. 76.
3. Ian Bradley, *The Celtic Way*, (Darton, Longman, Todd, 1996), p. 121.
4. Quoted from Ian Findlay in Michael Mitton's, *Soul of Celtic Spirituality in the Lives of Its Saints*. (Twenty-third Publications, 1996), p. 46.
5. *Ibid.*, p.47, quoting David Adam.
6. Esther de Waal, *Every Earthly Blessing*, (Servant Publications, 1992) p. 10-11.
7. David Adam, *The Edge of Glory*, (Triangle, 1985), p. 2.
8. David Adam, *The Cry of the Deer*, (Triangle, 1987), p. 28.
9. Noel Dermot O'Donoghue, *The Mountain Behind the Mountain*, (T & T Clark), p. ix.
10. *Ibid.*, p. 31.
11. David Adam, *The Cry of the Deer*, p. 75.
12. Esther de Waal, *Living with Contradiction*, (Harper and Row, 1989), p. 82.
13. Kathleen Norris, *Dakota: A Spiritual Geography*, (Houghton Mifflin, 1993), p. 121.
14. Michael Mitton, *Soul of Celtic Spirituality*, pp. 36-37.
15. Esther de Waal, *The Celtic Vision*, (St. Bede's Publications, 1988), p. 12.
16. Ian Bradley, p. 94.
17. *Ibid.*, p. 1.
18. *Ibid.*, p. 88.
19. Michael Mitton, p. 56.
20. Ian Bradley, p. 96.
21. Noel Dermot O'Donoghue, p. 57.
22. *Ibid.*, p. 58.
23. Philip Sheldrake, p. 58.
24. *Ibid.*, p. 59.
25. David Adam, *Tides and Seasons*, (Triangle, 1989), p. 29.
26. John J. O'Riordain, C.Ss.R., *The Music of What Happens*, (St. Mary's Press, 1996), p. 69.
27. Noel Dermot O'Donoghue, p. 51.